MOTHER WORE COMBAT BOOTS

The Author, 1945

MOTHER WORE COMBAT BOOTS

And Chased Troop Trains

A young woman's adventure story as an Army
nurse in World War II

by

Meredith Miller Matthews

Grapevine Press
Akron, Ohio

THIS BOOK IS DEDICATED TO

My dear James; husband, friend, lover

and

our wonderful children
Timothy, Clarissa, Theodore

Pledge of the Army Nurse

As an Army nurse, I accept the
responsibilities of an
officer in the Army Nurse Corps.

I shall give faithful care to the men
who fight for the freedom of this
Country and to the women who stand
behind them.

I shall bring to the American soldier
wherever he may be
the best of my knowledge and
professional skill.

I shall approach him cheerfully at all
times under any conditions I may find.

I shall endeavor to maintain the
highest nursing standards possible in
the performance of my duties.

I shall appear fearless in the presence
of danger and
quiet the fears of others to the best
of my ability.

My only criticism shall be
constructive. The reputation and good
name of the Army Nurse Corps and of
the nursing profession shall be
uppermost in my thoughts, second
only to the care of my patients.

I shall endeavor to be a credit to my
Country and to the uniform I wear.

TABLE OF CONTENTS

PREFACE -- XI

INTRODUCTION ------------------------------------- XVII

ACKNOWLEDGEMENTS ---------------------------- XXI

PROLOGUE
    Die Casting -- 1

I   WAR CLOUDS ----------------------------------- 7

II   THE PHYSICAL ------------------------------- 13

III YOU'RE in the ARMY NOW ----------------- 15

IV   STATESIDE
    Basic Train1ng ------------------------------ 17
    Newton D. Baker --------------------------- 25
    The Troop Train ---------------------------- 36
    California, Here I Come ------------------- 39
    Point of Embarkation ---------------------- 43

V   THE CROSSING ----------------------------- 46

VI   THE PHILIPPINES
    Manila Bay --------------------------------- 52
    Novaliches --------------------------------- 54
    The Palace --------------------------------- 68
    The Surrender ----------------------------- 72
    The Blue-eyed Colonel ------------------- 78
    Leyte --------------------------------------- 86

VII JAPAN.
    "East is East" ------------------------------ 102
    The 128th Station Hospital --------------- 106
    The 334th Station Hospital --------------- 122
    The Old Schoolhouse --------------------- 144

VIII HOMEWARD 152

EPILOGUE
      Vintage Wine 163

END NOTES 172

DOCUMENTS 174

PREFACE

On October 28, 1989, I was privileged to attend the first reunion of women veterans of World War II. I was very impressed by the many contributions of the 350,000 women who served, and although I am numbered among them, I had no knowledge of the scope of our participation in the war.

I submit the following pages that were written by Dr. Evelyn M. Monahan of Atlanta, Georgia for the attendees to the reunion. The National Women Veterans Foundation, of which Dr. Monahan was Vice President and Director, Special Projects, was the sponsor of the event.

I have made it a project of mine to pass out copies of "Who Will Remember?" to every group to whom I have spoken.

(The following material, "Who Will Remember?", is used with the permission of Dr. Evelyn M. Monahan.)

Who will remember?

On October 28, 1989, the first national event to honor women veterans of World War II will take place at the Georgia World Congress Center in Atlanta, Georgia.

The National Women Veterans Foundation has received thousands of letters from women veterans of World War II commending the event and stating plans to attend.

The Foundation has also received many letters from male veterans who want to make sure their wives, sisters, mothers, aunts or friends are included in the "Salute." And we have received more than 100 calls and letters from men whose deceased wives and relatives served in World War II—they plan to attend the "Salute" in place of the deceased women.

Who will remember?

The servicewomen of World War II all volunteered to serve their country. Many won Silver Stars, Bronze Stars, Purple Hearts and dozens of other medals and decorations. But they never asked for one ribbon, one medal or one salute.

Now we ask for them in the name of justice and honor.

These women are just as much national heroes as the men who wore their country's uniform into battle. Unfortunately, their modesty and reticence has made it easy for the nation to overlook their contribution to victory.

There is no more unassuming group of human beings in the world than the women who served in World War II.

However, time is growing short. These WWII servicewomen speak of their dwindling numbers. Friends and comrades have died in recent years. "Buddies" who used to exchange Christmas cards each year—cards that no longer arrive to cheer the season.

These women speak of their concern that no one will care about their service after they have gone. They ask the heartfelt question, "Who will remember?"

Who will remember?...

....the young women—Army and Navy nurses—who were captured when Bataan and Corregidor fell?

....Or the more than 100 brave women who were prisoners of war for almost 37 months?

Who will remember?...

....the women of the Signal Corps who stayed at their posts in Africa, England, France and Italy despite enemy bombing and fire?

....Or that they maintained communications links vital to American lives and victories?

Who will remember?...

....the women of the Transportation Corps who drove trucks loaded with explosives and ammunition along crater pitted roads bringing vital supplies to our fighting men?

....Or the women who coordinated the troop and supply trains essential to our final victory?

Who will remember?...

....the countless nurses who were bombed and strafed while caring for the brave young men of our armed forces?

Who will remember?...

....the nurses who sailed on unescorted hospital ship—lighted white targets for enemy forces?

....Or the six young Army nurses killed by enemy fire at Anzio?

....Or the nurses killed when the hospital ship Comfort was sunk?

....Or the Army nurses who were wounded when the hospital ship New Foundland was bombed?

Who will remember?...

....the two young Army nurses—sisters—who won Purple Hearts when they were wounded in their sleep off Sicily by enemy bombs which flung them up into the humid night air and back again to the deck of their ship?

Who will remember?...

....the women who served as cryptographers and intelligence officers in every theater of war?

....Or the young female Army officer who traveled for two days to deliver an "eyes only" message to General George Patton?

Who will remember?...

....the women who delivered countless "eyes only" messages to General Omar Bradley, General Montgomery and many other field commanders?

Who will remember?...

...the Navy nurses flown into Iwo Jima, Guadalacanal and Okinawa while the battles still raged?

....Or the solemn recognition of their situation when they learned the Marine Corpsmen on board were armed with orders to shoot them if the evacuation planes were captured?

Who will remember?...

....the young women Marines who risked their lives to save fellow Marines from a death dealing fire?

....Or the women Marines who went willingly to every duty station to which the Corps sent them?

Who will remember?...

....the WAVES who kept their country's top secrets and directed shelling and bombing with the intelligence reports they gathered and delivered?

Who will remember?...

....the SPARS, willing to put duty first on any assignment—willing to go without question or complaint to where their country sent them?

Who will remember?...

.... the WASPS who ferried all types of military planes to bases in the United States and foreign countries—a mission in which 38 gave their lives?

Who will remember?...

....the WAC who won a Bronze Star and five battle stars for her service in New Guinea, Leyte, the Philippines and Okinawa?

....Or the jungle rot and Dinge fever she suffered doing her job?

Who will remember?...

....the WAACs, WACs, WAVES, SPARS and the women Marines who worked in ammunition dumps, motor pools, air traffic towers, link trainers at aerial guns and American and Allied troops training centers?

Who will remember?...

....the women who taught men how to fly?

Who will remember?...

....the women who taught men aerial gunnery?

....Or women test pilots and pioneers for new weapons that helped speed their country's victory?

....the women who endured the heat and miserable conditions of New Guinea, New Caledonia, Saipan, Burma, India, Africa, Guam, Guadalcanal, Iwo Jima and Okinawa?

Who will remember?...

....the women who shivered alongside the men in England, France, Germany and Belgium?

....Or who lived in ankle deep mud and suffered weevils in their meager food supply?

....Or those who often lived on one canteen of water per day?

....Or those who endured frequent enemy bombing?

Who will remember? ..

.... that thousands of the grandmothers of today were the soldiers, sailors, SPARS and Marines of World War II?

....Or that the hands guiding young children through fast food lines and amusement parks today are the hands that soothed the wounded soldier, sailor and marines of yesterday?

....And are the hands that passed ammunition, first aid and secret codes?

Who will remember?...

....You and I must be the living response to that question. These women have written a proud and honorable History—it is up to you and me to give that History a voice.

If you and I do not remember, the world itself will forget!

INTRODUCTION

For some time, I have wanted to record my experiences as an army nurse during World War II. I have felt a need to leave a journal for my progeny so that they may know me as someone other than their mother; someone who contributed to her home, church, community and beyond; someone who fulfilled the destiny of her species as a wife and mother; someone who continues to reach for maturity as she copes with the vicissitudes of the geriatric scene. I am playing out the role in the final act of my life span with my usual fortitude and, yes, enjoyment.

I had the privilege of caring for my aged parents in their dotage, learning who they were from a perspective other than "Mom and Dad". Although the phenomena has been denied in print (no doubt by someone younger who hasn't been there yet), I was strapped into the "sandwich generation" forever switching gears between four generations. My journal has been on the back burner until now. This is the time. My responsibilities to my generations have dissolved, and I have this window of opportunity before I get into my own dotage.

The interest generated by the fifty year commemorations of the "last" great war spurred my recollections of my involvement in it. It became expedient to capture these memories inasmuch as I was invited as a guest speaker for several church groups and antique clubs. The resulting outline that evolved encouraged me to proceed.

I have discovered in consulting other veterans that no two people relay the same event with any consistency of detail. A hundred people will tell a hundred tales of an event, each colored by his or her prior conditioning with emphasis determined by individual bias. If one could line up all the stories, a truer, broader picture of the event would emerge.

For example: Within my story is a description of Manila as I saw it. My dear friend, Clenie, whom I mention herein, told me of her glimpse of Manila that included hotels, theater, and night life, quite different from the Manila I saw. We are both right.

Each one of us traveled a very narrow line in the performance of our duty. We were not privy to the war room with its panoramic vision of the larger operation. We were not in a need to know position. We were not informed enough to see the epic proportions of a great effort of which we were a small part. The colossal endeavor, then, that was World War II must be reduced to its component parts, the individuals.

So it is that I tell my story as I lived it and remembered it, some of it clouded by time, and some of it as vivid as if it were still unfolding. I have been frustrated by my failure to locate the letters I wrote to my family. They were documentary in nature and would have been a valuable resource. I have tried to reconstruct the gaps in my memory by availing myself of the military archives in College Park, Maryland and the archives at Carlisle Barracks, Carlisle, Pennsylvania.

This is not a definitive history. Rather, it is a young woman's adventure story. It is intimate and personal, and it details experiences that coil around events of 1945 and 1946. Actually, one could say that this story is written by two people; one, an eager young woman with a passion for life, and the other, a more mellow, reflective older woman. The older one cannot refrain from commentary that reflects the experience and wisdom gained from her sojourn on this planet. The younger one still has spasms of growing pains, but she matures considerably as the tale unfolds.

I have wrestled with the subject of frankness, but considering that today's world is more shock proof than my world of fifty years ago, I do not think that anything I say about the customs and mores of my youth will offend anyone. To today's generations, I say there is nothing new under the sun, but the emphasis, the propriety, and the numerical incidences of lapses in taboos are different. Each era must be looked at from the perspective of its own time frame.

The title, "MOTHER WORE COMBAT BOOTS" (and chased troop trains), was, in World War II, a disparaging remark used to insult as in, "Aw, your mother wears combat boots etc.", but I did wear combat boots and, on one occasion, I did chase a troop train. When referring to my friends, I use only first names.

Although I do not take myself seriously, I am not comfortable writing in the first person, but if I am going to pen my story, I will have to overcome any self-consciousness talking about me.

I cannot claim a "first" in service - as in first woman this or first woman that. I, and many like me, were "casuals" whose duty it was to replace the women who badly needed relief. I was dedicated, patriotic, and proud of my contribution ....and I still am.

Histories documenting the contributions of women in our nation's conflicts from the Revolutionary War to the present have been exceedingly sparse because they were not written by our gender. The paucity of literature highlighting our partnership with our men is being rectified by the many books now in print by women veterans. My fantasy is that the following story will be included in the illustrious company of publications by America's Lady Vets.

ACKNOWLEDGEMENTS

I gratefully acknowledge:

Inez Clendenin Myers, dear friend and classmate, who has aided in orienting me to the broader picture of events in the Philippines and Japan, and who encouraged me to write this story.

Thelma Schmitt Robinson, dear friend and classmate, who has corrected some earlier misconceptions that helped insure greater accuracy on some salient facts of this story.

The research department of the Akron/Summit County library which has patiently researched and answered many diverse questions.

The Military Archives at Carlisle Barracks, Carlisle, Pennsylvania for their guidance.

The Military Archives at College Park, Maryland for their guidance

Myrl Jean Hughes, of Hendersonville, North Carolina, who was formerly attached to the 334th Station Hospital in Hollandia, Dutch New Guinea, for providing me with a valuable history of the 334th.

The willing attention of General Wilma Vaught (Ret.), President of the Women in Military Service of America (WIMSA), and Lt.Col. Marilla Cushman (Ret.), Director of Public Relations and Development, for putting me in touch with Col. Ruby Sellars (Ret.) who is field representative of WIMSA in Atlanta Georgia. On my behalf, Ms. Sellars put me in touch with the author of the "Who Will Remember ?" piece in the preface, Dr. Evelyn M. Monahan of Atlanta, Georgia.

To my patient, encouraging husband, James, who subsisted on
TV dinners while I was molding and refining my story.

To my daughter, Clarissa, who failing to teach her mother to
be computer literate, performed all the computer chores for this
book.

PROLOGUE

Die Casting

For me, life is not a spectator sport. I can dip back into the deepest pool of my memory and still feel the zest and heady exhilaration of being in the middle of a game, a play, an organization or an experiment. Never satisfied to be on the fringes of life, I participated fully, not for recognition or power, but because of interest and curiosity. And, something more. I always had an abiding desire to be of service. My generation was one of dependability and responsibility, and I took the charge seriously.

Though I came across as a high profile achiever, there were other less obvious facets: empathy, sympathy and compassion. I was, and still am, a very private person. I have been burdened with such an extreme sensibility and respect for all of God's critters as to constitute a handicap.

The die was cast early for my future career. My father was a physician and my mother was a nurse. My maternal grandmother inadvertently reinforced my natural inclination by making miniature nurse uniforms for my sister and me. In our uniforms, we tended our dolls in the back yard rose arbor. We had the healthiest dolls in the neighborhood.

Ours was a conventional middle class family. Father practiced his profession during the depths of the depression. Everyone in our neighborhood was unemployed, but Father worked in a haze of exhaustion. He was a pediatrician, and babies and children still got sick.

Our neighborhood, Firestone Park, was built by the rubber magnate, Harvey S. Firestone, to house his workers who worked at the nearby Firestone Tire and Rubber Factory, now called Bridgestone, a Japanese firm. When the factories were humming, and a southerly breeze was blowing, the area had a distinct burnt rubber odor. That is why the west side of town became more fashionable than Firestone Park. Now, however, the factories were mute and cold, and the whole area was idle.

Father had a Model A Ford car because doctors made house calls. His patients paid him with whatever they could afford, and he would come home with beets, potatoes and carrots from their gardens. Sometimes, he was hard pressed to buy gasoline for the car because carrots for currency were unacceptable.

But the whole neighborhood loved his car - the children that is. Children were the chief crop on our block, and we would all turn out to grab a footing on the running boards of his car when he headed off to make his morning rounds. Now Father was a very reserved, formal man. His dignity and professionalism were such as to make him forbidding. However, his demeanor never deterred those of us who grabbed a spot on the running boards. Hanging on for dear life, our hair streaming behind, the cold air in our face, we knew we were having the thrill of our life, while Father was sputtering in embarrassment and frustration at the hoydens whose unbridled glee shattered his poise.

Mother was in the first graduating class from Mt. Sinai Hospital in Cleveland, Ohio. She was a tall, slim, beautiful blond, with a "Scarlett O'Hara"[1] waistline and her pale, fragile beauty belied her strength. She and one other girl were the only ones in the hospital who did not succumb to the pandemic influenza outbreak of 1918 and 1919.

Mother was gentle and feminine, the consummate lady, and I adored her. She was considerate and caring, and her genteel qualities made her loved by all whose lives she touched. She had a way of chastising so that one did not realize one was being disciplined. She worked hard on civilizing and domesticating her middle child, but, alas, said child was not a lady. She climbed trees, played football, and learned to wrestle and box. To Mother's dismay, the latter two skills were fostered by Father.

Father had graduated from West Point during World War I. In his plebe days, Dwight Eisenhower was an upper classman. Following overseas service in WWI, he continued his role as an officer in the peacetime army. He and mother were married by then, and both tried valiantly to adjust to army life. However, both were too mid-Victorian to accept the Roaring Twenties that had burst upon the scene. The women smoked, bobbed their hair, and wore short skirts. The environment was like a playground. Both had brought into their union the ingrained seeds of service to others, and those seeds had to be nourished. So it was with reluctance that Father resigned his commission and began casting about for his place in the sun. It was Mother who steered him into medicine. He had found his niche.

It was Father's West Point training in boxing and wrestling that he imparted to me. Like most men of the day, he wanted a son. I was the second of two daughters, and, in lieu of a son, he would pass those skills on to me. I reveled in it. I was the logical choice. Mother's success with teaching ladylike behavior to my sister was diluted by her miserable failure with me. I had a whole wardrobe of knickers that Mrs. Thomas across the street had handed down to me from one of her sons. Knickers were those trousers that bloused just below the knee and were met at that juncture by long argyle socks. Young ladies did not wear trousers, and I had no knowledge of slacks and jeans that would one day be standard fashion. No matter. I had my knickers, and I donned them immediately upon my return home from school. I became so good at wrestling that I bested every boy on the block. My mother despaired. This recalcitrant child would never be a credit to her family. In fact, in any neighborhood fracas, the local gossips would say that they knew that the elder, Catherine, didn't do it. She was too much of a lady. So it automatically followed that that naughty Meredith Miller was the guilty party.

So I passed my childhood. I was happy. None of us who congregated on the street every day to play ball (there weren't many cars in those days) or to play hopscotch, Simon Says, kick-the-can or jacks knew we were deprived. We did not miss what we did not have. Adults handled adult problems in those days and tried to give us as normal a childhood as possible. Our meals were sometimes lacking in quantity and variety, but we shared whatever we had. Mother fed every hobo who came to her door. It might have been nothing more than catsup soup, molasses bread and hot coffee, but they were never turned away. We lived in the middle of the block. These hungry men would zero in on our house. Was our house marked? I had heard that it was so. I used to stand in front of my house and scrutinize it carefully, but I could never find the identifying mark.

I was ten when I got a baby brother and Father got his son. I virtually swiped him from Mother and bathed him, fed him, took him out in his buggy, and rocked him to sleep. No one else on the block had a real live doll to mother. I saw no incongruity between caring for my baby brother and playing football or wrestling.

I was growing up. I felt a bit of nagging anxiety because I was changing. I was more reflective, more contemplative. I was losing interest in chasing the ice man's truck to grab ice chunks to suck on a hot summer day. He came every day with his big tongs which he would impale in a twenty-five pound square of ice. Then he would hoist the block of ice up on his leather padded shoulder and carry it to the ice box on the back porch of our house.

I still watched for the milk man's horse though. I could pet him and nuzzle him while the milk man delivered milk to Mother and the other ladies. Still, I wasn't playing kick-the-can with the same enthusiasm. I was seeing my surroundings in a new dimension. I loved my street. It was bordered on both sides by tall elms that arched over the street, meeting each other in the middle. I thought I was in a cathedral. With my book in hand, I was accustomed to climbing a certain tree and settling into a high crotch concealed from the world by the dense foliage. My tree was growing too.

When I visited my street in later years, I found it all naked and stark. My cathedral was gone. All the elms on my street and the whole city were felled because of an infestation of the Dutch elm disease.

I had made an uneasy truce between the tomboy and the acknowledgement that I was a girl-child. About this time, I remember arguing vehemently with one of the neighborhood boys that one day women were going to West Point. That radical concept bordered on heresy. We were on the swing in the back yard rose arbor, and the more adamantly I defended my position, the more furiously the swing rocked and creaked on its chains. I knew with the certainty of life itself that my prophesy would come true, maybe too late for me, but I would see it happen.

The depression must have been easing because I got my first new coat. The dog almost attacked me because he only knew the girl with the old green hand-me-down. We had a succession of dogs because Father's patients honored him with their dogs in lieu of payment. The ones that donated their dogs were unable to feed them and they hoped that by giving them to their doctor, the animals would have a good home. Of course they got a good home. A serious consideration, though, was that my parents had to find a solution to the feeding problem.

I was fast approaching puberty. My dreams of achieving my mother's statuesque height dissolved when I ended my growth spurt with a puny five feet, three inches. I felt stunted. But I was strong, I reminded myself! I used to call myself the "Great Katrinka" after a big bruiser of a woman in the comic strip, "The Toonerville Folks" [2]. In the story, "Katrinka" was always hoisting the Toonerville Trolley back on the track. "Katrinka" was my alter ego, and she showed up from time to time when I needed her.

Years later, my self-image changed when I discovered why my clothes were always too large. I had been buying clothes for "Katrinka" instead of me.

But, the vague anxieties persisted.

Meredith   Catherine

In our nurses' uniforms, we tended our dolls in the backyard rose arbor. We had the healthiest dolls in the neighborhood.

WAR CLOUDS

When I was thirteen, I became aware of what was euphemistically referred to as "War Clouds". I was in the eighth grade of school, and although I had blossomed rapidly, I was loathe to give up the last vestiges of childhood. A school chum and I had a contest to see who could eat the most and gain the most weight the fastest. I won. I still changed into my knickers after school, outgrown by now, and headed out for football or bicycling.

I had insisted on a boy's bike, and after years of pleading, I finally was rewarded one Christmas morning. Our neighborhood had a disparity between children and bikes. That problem was solved by having the "bikeless" ride on the saddle of the "bikees". A massive swarm of bikers would gear up in the morning for a thirty to forty mile trip around the city and parks. One of the "bikeless", Donnie, would ride on the saddle of my bike, and I would pump the whole course standing up with Donnie's arms around my waist.

I was disturbed by the pleasant feeling I experienced by having Donnie so close. After all, I hated boys, ugh. They were only good for wrestling or football. With tomboy contempt, I eschewed silk stockings, cosmetics, "fussy" dresses. Also, I vowed that I would never, no, never marry! And I vowed that I would never, no, never have babies!

But as I coped with the strange new changes of mind and body, something far more sinister was licking at the edges of my consciousness. Subdued conversations by my parents at night; an unnamed agitation permeating the air at adult gatherings, but I would try to banish the uneasiness. After all, what pubescent girl really was interested in anything except the comics and, possibly, boys? My parents habitually shielded us from their concerns, but that did not assuage my apprehension. I sensed, rather than knew, that some calamity was casting clouds on my sunny horizon. I never discussed my dark forebodings with anyone, but I prayed that whatever this thing was, it would go away before my friends were faced with it.

I was fifteen and in high school in 1938 when Hitler invaded Austria and then Czechoslovakia. I tried to relegate my concerns to a subliminal level. It was incumbent on me to concentrate on my job, that of studying and graduating, participating and contributing. No organization was out of reach from Latin Club, Blue-Tri, Sub-Deb Club, Red Cross to Rifle Club, A Capella Choir and National Honor Society. No one ever told me that to get through life I had to "feel good"; that as long as I "felt good" about myself and had "self-esteem", that was an achievement, and I was a success.

What I was told was that I had a job to do; that I must apply myself and complete my job to the best of my ability; that I must do my job with honor, and as a result of my measurable accomplishments, I would have concrete evidence of the fruits of my labor. And with that kind of productivity, I would, undoubtedly, "feel good". Inculcated with the foregoing principles, I had always been a good student and a quick study despite my over involvement in extra-curricular activities and dating.

Yes, I was dating. The tomboy reluctantly had grown up. One's first date is a milestone. I was thirteen and was coerced into accepting an invitation from the son of one of Mother's friends. I detected matchmaking at work. I was invited to a wrestling match which made the whole episode more palatable. My swain's grandmother was scandalized. Disapproving, she said, "In my day, a gentleman took a young lady to the theater or a ball. But a wrestling match?" In preparation for my ordeal, I got in the tub and scoured myself vigorously with "Lifebuoy"[3] soap. Dressed and ready, I presented myself to Mother for inspection. I shone like a beacon, smelled like a medicine chest and was the color of the soap, lobster red. Poor Mother, her shoulders sagged. Would this daughter ever be presentable enough to attract a suitable beau? She needn't have worried.

One of our math teachers was a World War I veteran. He wanted to start a rifle club. It would be part of the athletic program, and its members would be eligible for varsity letters. He had two daughters. He would establish a girls' rifle team. It was in the Rifle Club that I learned how to shoot.

Father was not going to start me out on a big, fancy gun with sophisticated sights. He bought me a single shot, bolt action Winchester 22 with a simple v-notch sight. The Winchester was so light that I couldn't hold it steady. That is when I learned to sway with it and squeeze the trigger the split second it was on the bull's eye. The same procedure was applicable on a gun that was too heavy for me. All of us in the club became crack shots, so much so that we won every match. Since we were the only girls' team in the city, we were always pitted against the boys' rifle clubs. It was great training.

It was in the rifle club that I met Clenie. We have had parallel lives ever since.

It was in high school that I had my first brush with politics. My school had placed me in contention for the presidency of the city wide American Red Cross. All the candidates had to campaign and give political speeches. When we met in a large auditorium for the final campaign speech before a gathering of all the delegates from the individual schools, I realized for the first time that I was the only girl running for office. I had already decided that I didn't like politics, but my school was counting on me so I would do my best. I won. Such hoopla! After many years, the title had returned to the girls.

And so my high school years sped by. Immediately, I went off to college. I was a young woman in a hurry. I had enrolled in Akron University before my high school graduation ceremonies had taken place. By doubling up on courses and attending classes from June of 1940 through August of 1941, I had accrued in excess of two years' worth of credit hours.

In September of 1940, The Selective Service Training Act was passed over the objections of the church, labor, educators and organized pacifists. It was the first peacetime military conscription in the nation's history, its urgency predicated on the government's recognition of the imminence of war. After the attack on Pearl Harbor on December 7, 1941, an amendment to the Act raised the draft registration age to include men from eighteen to sixty-four.

Some of my high school boys had enlisted in 1940, bragging that they would get their compulsory year of service over with and get a "jump start" on college. It was daunting for them to realize that, as a result of our entrance into the war in December of 1941, their year would be extended for the duration, many to serve through 1945.

My father felt a strong sense of duty to enlist and offer his services as a medical officer. He was already forty-seven years old in 1941. His family urged him to stay and hold down the home front. He worked very hard those war years caring for the civilian population.

In college, I joined a sorority. I tried to fit in, but I was disillusioned by what I deemed was the trivializing of the college experience. The Student Center was always brimming with students playing bridge, drinking cokes and cutting classes. I felt that my time could be better spent in situations where I would be of service to somebody. My earlier instincts of nurturing and caring had come to the fore.

I entered Akron City Hospital School of Nursing in the fall of 1941. I couldn't get out of training fast enough. By my junior year, the young men who came to call were already in uniform. The interns and residents would go into military service upon completion of their training at Akron City, and by my senior year, the government was talking about drafting nurses. To alleviate the shortage and to free state-side nurses for overseas duty, the Cadet Nurse Corps was formed. It was a program whereby senior student nurses would be assigned to service hospitals to care for the wounded. They would receive full academic credit applied toward graduation. A condition was a pledge to join the armed forces after graduation.

The whole senior class enrolled in the cadet program save eight of us. I was one of the holdouts. My rebelliousness had reared its stubborn head. It wasn't that I disapproved the program, or that I hadn't planned from the beginning to join the army. In some perverse way, I wanted my enlistment to be on my own terms, devoid of any conditions. This quirk of mine was to get me in trouble later on. My defense has always been that I was true to myself, some times at my expense.

While a nursing student, I saw the introduction of penicillin. I participated in experimental treatments for burn patients, treatments being tried at the behest of the army, the protocol of which would be used in the field. I made many enduring friendships. I even wrote poetry while I kept a lonely night vigil in surgery, autoclaving instrument packs and stocking the operating rooms for the following day's surgery schedule.

At last, graduation! State Boards! Making up sick time before I could don my whites. And I enlisted in the army.

It is a tribute to our people how they emerged from a demoralizing and enervating depression to galvanize the home front into gearing for a war production that far exceeded the necessary quotas.

Our country has never faced a challenge with the same solidarity since. Wars are not just, some less so than others, but World War II had to be fought. Our men, fighting on two fronts, were not debating the merits of this conflict. They only knew that Hitler must be stopped in Europe, and Tojo had to be held at bay in the Pacific. We, as a nation, have been so very, very lucky. We have not suffered a brutal occupation by a conqueror or the devastation of our lands and cities. It grieves me that our children know so little about this conflict or the valiant sacrifices made by our military and homefront.

Early in 1995, my husband and I went to the military archives in Suitland, Maryland outside of Washington D.C. He had hoped to find after-action reports pertinent to times and places surrounding personal traumas that he needed to clarify. While there, we met a young, thirty-three year old man who was very helpful to us. He had been researching data pertaining to his father and uncles. With an insight usually alien to one his age, he said, "Your generation was born with a fire in its belly." He contended that our generation was no accident. We were molded in the depression and then tempered to bright hardness. He opined that he feared his generation would not be up to the challenges that we faced. I pray that he is wrong. (In 1996, the archives moved to magnificent new facilities in College Park, Maryland. It is reputed to be the largest such facility in the world.

At last! Graduation and I could don my "whites"!

THE PHYSICAL

We took our army physicals at Crile Veterans Hospital in Cleveland, Ohio. Crile was named after one of the world's great surgeons, George Washington Crile. He studied at Western Reserve University and Vienna, London and Paris. He built up an enormous practice in Cleveland where he was also a professor of many disciplines at Wooster and Western Reserve Universities. Among many pioneering procedures, he performed the first direct blood transfusion and originated block anesthesia.

Nearly all of the seventy-five graduates of our nursing class opted for one of the armed service branches. We army enlistees trooped, en masse, to Crile. There we donned hospital gowns, stood in queues in the halls waiting our turn to be summoned by different doctors, each of whom handled various and sundry parts of us, and each in his own room.

I was healthy and strong, but two minor flaws might influence the outcome of my physical; one being ridiculously low blood pressure and the other being severe menstrual cramps. Nothing was going to stop me from being an army nurse. I had "champed the bit" too long to be deterred now. I recall jogging in place vigorously outside the door of the blood pressure man. This effort had managed to elevate my pressure to 106/70. Then to the menstrual cramp man, no doubt an OB/GYN doctor. To his query of whether or not I suffered from cramps, I avowed, "No! Never!" That lie was to come back to haunt me.

The last room was the psychiatrist's inner sanctum. One beautiful, fragile young woman with large luminous eyes that reminded me of a frightened deer failed her psychiatric exam. When I entered his room, I was taken aback to see him lolling, indolently, in his chair listening to music through ear phones. I acknowledge that giving army physicals was a pretty boring way to practice one's specialty, but couldn't he see? This was important to me. He barely slid his ear phones off one ear and asked, "What would you do if I turned you down in your desire to enlist?" He hadn't brought out the best in me, and I shot back with the quip, "I'd be a psychiatrist just like you." He hastened my exit with, "Get outta here."

Two of my classmates and dearest friends would be going with me, Clenie and Schmitty. Clenie and I had been corrupted in a hurry, becoming habituated to nicotine with what had innocently started out as curiosity. Not wishing to divulge our very private reasons for joining the army, she and I told everyone that we had enlisted to get cigarettes. There was an endless supply of name-brand poison allocated to the armed forces. One of my greatest victories was banishing the habit.

We needed only to wait for orders informing us when and where to report for duty.

YOU'RE in the ARMY NOW

Much of what ensued with unnerving rapidity is a blur. The events surrounding my service career can best be likened to an early jerky movie interspersed with Technicolor vignettes.

I continued to work at Akron City Hospital as I waited for my orders to report for active duty. I had chosen, as my first graduate duty, a ward fraught with challenge to my acumen and ingenuity. The sick and downtrodden who peopled my ward were the criminals, the gun shot wounds, the racial stabbings, the prostitutes, the central nervous system syphilis victims, the homeless habitues of the hobo jungles, and the indigent people who had no place else to go. The ward was an excellent training ground for any future duty.

I cut my hair short and had a tight permanent. It would be long and in pigtails ere I saw home again.

I was feted with going away parties. One of mother's friends put an embarrassing blurb in the local paper singling me out as a sort of Jeanne d'Arc.

My little brother, so proud of his big sister, put a blue star in the window. Remember? The blue star for a family member in the service; the gold star for death, the ultimate sacrifice?

I recall my parents' devastation, and, only in the years of my own parenthood, could I understand their fierce parental protectiveness of their cub. Yet, here was a circumstance about which they could do nothing. With youth, reckless and thoughtless, it has been forever thus. Their cub was leaving for the unknown.

Our adventure began March 1, 1945. Those of us who had enlisted together comprised the group that congregated at Akron's decrepit old train station, the facility that was an embarrassment to the city fathers. Notwithstanding an undercurrent of excitement, we were a solemn bunch. We resembled any diverse gathering of enlistees, male or female. We stood around in clusters with our parents who were striving for a nonchalance they didn't quite master.

The familiar scene had repeated itself thousands of times in every city and village throughout the country; that of parents trying not to play to any grief they might have felt, and of their sons and daughters faking a mien of false bravado. We boarded the train.

Clenie's father boarded with us for one last goodbye to his only child. Before he could disembark, the train chugged out of the station. We were hysterical at his dilemma. We had needed that moment of levity.

Our destination: Ft. Benjamin Harrison, Indianapolis, Indiana.

STATESIDE

Basic Training

The train rolled to a halt next to a vacant field. There, we detrained with all our luggage and milled around hesitantly questioning our next move. No one had the temerity to take charge. Take charge of what? We could see Ft. Benjamin Harrison in the distance, but our enterprise did not extend to hiking there. Did all new arrivals get the same reception? At the verge of thinking we had mistaken the date, we saw a bus approaching the field. Without protest, we climbed aboard. This would be the first of many times that self-determination would bow to the army overseer of all logistics.

The next few days sped by in a dizzying Maelstrom[4] of activity. We were fed and billeted. We received our uniform allowance and purchased all our wardrobe from dress uniforms, duty uniforms to calisthenics garb. We were assigned to platoons, given orientation, introduced to our drill sergeant, and finally, had our inoculations, known to all as "shots". For the most part, I do not remember such mundane things as eating and sleeping unless some other important happening is connected with those instinctive activities.

I remember the shots, though, not because they caused any particular jolt, but because of the rumors they generated when we learned that, in addition to the usual, they included cholera and bubonic plague. Where were we going? To need cholera and plague shots?

Our arms were very sore from the shots. I was chagrined at the girls that whimpered and whined that they simply couldn't take calisthenics; they would have to warm the sidelines; their arms hurt too much. Our "cute, blue-eyed drill sergeant" (as we had nicknamed him) didn't succumb to their wheedling and made them do calisthenics with lots of arm exercises. As for me, I had not learned the word "macho" yet, but I guess the label fit.

Our day started with a gun salvo at 5:30 AM followed, at 6:00 AM, by calisthenics, marching and close-order drill. To the derision of some of my less "macho" comrades, I loved calisthenics and close-order drill. These exercises had the added benefit of being excellent mental gymnastics. It distressed me when some dilettante was responsible for making our platoon look like something out of "Gomer Pyle"[5].

The balance of each day was spent at the base hospital, Billings General Hospital, on ward duty. It was our initiation to the care of the wounded. I recall one soldier whose whole torso had been raked with machine gun fire. Although he was critically ill, the bullets had missed his vital organs.

The days of basic training passed with their exhausting routine and deep, dreamless nights. We were learning the main tenets of army life, i.e. rumors, "hurry-up-and-wait" , and griping. I griped about the gripers. The rumors were generated by the fact that we were never told anything so we manufactured logical scenarios. "Hurry-up-and-wait" was a peculiar condition suffered by most of us whereby orders from "above" were issued calling for rapid deployment to stem some emergency, and when we arrived "there", no one knew what to do with us. So we would wait....and wait. Griping must have been a God given prerogative because the armed forces thrived on it and did it well.

I had been in basic less than a week when I received a summons from the Akron courts ordering me to come and give a deposition detailing my involvement in a fatal accident on the previous New Year's Eve.

> New Year's Eve has been bad karma for me. I should huddle safely indoors until it is over. During my early dating years, I was not allowed to go out on that night. Later, I was permitted to venture forth, but my curfew was midnight and not a second after. On the only December 31 that I was enjoying a genuine celebration, my escort's car was rammed from behind by an inebriated reveler as we were stopped for a traffic light.
>
> On the New Year's Eve for which I had received the summons, I had been working the 3:00 to 11:00 shift. It had been a difficult night with fights, stabbings and accidents amidst the celebrants, making for many additional admissions to my floor. I

finally made it off duty in time to catch the last bus home at 1:00AM.

I was dozing when a violent crash whipped me out of my seat and threw me forward under the bus driver's feet. I was stunned, but I remember his crawling over me and off the bus. I struggled up and made my way outside. There I saw a demolished convertible that had hit the bus with such force that the bus had careened up an embankment and come to a stop in the front yard of a residence, narrowly missing the house.

I immediately went to the car to see if I could be of any assistance. A man was wandering around dazed. From the strong liquor odor on him, one could assume that he was "allegedly" drunk. I went to his wife who was on the passenger side of the front seat. I couldn't do anything for her. The crash had killed her. I still remember her party dress and how pretty she was. The police, having arrived, took my name and address, and I faded from the scene of flashing lights, sirens and noise and walked the rest of the way home. I had plenty of time on my solo walk in the middle of the night to ponder those new admissions to my ward, folks who were bent on self-destruction, and to reflect on the man whose wife I had just pronounced dead. I decided that the eve of a new year was a jinx, and I would have nothing more to do with it. Much later, in Japan, that jinx theory was reinforced when the jeep in which I was riding had an accident on - what else? - New Year's Eve.

I was naive about army protocol. I took my court summons to the Chief Nurse. She had told me that the army always tries to cooperate with civilian authority and that I should check with the fort commander. He had said that, yes, it was fine to leave to satisfy the summons. So, I left!

Talk about "Innocents Abroad"![6] I boarded a train for home. On the journey, military police (M.P.s) patrolled the civilian trains, doubling back through the cars after every stop, checking and rechecking every soldier's orders. When they came to me, they would tip their hats with a greeting such as "Good morning, Ma'am." I did not have to be a genius to realize that I would be in major trouble if one of the army police asked for my orders. I didn't have any! So that's how the military operates? Ohmygosh! With sudden clarity, I realized that I was AWOL (Absent Without Leave). I had not waited for orders to be cut authorizing my absence from the fort.

Once in Akron, I popped in to say "Hi!" to Mom and Dad, rushed to the court house to give my deposition and caught the next train back to camp. Maybe if I hurried, I wouldn't be missed. It was not to be.

Train connections on the return trip were erratic, and I found myself in some nameless little town with a lengthy lay-over. The hours inched on into the middle of the night. I considered stretching out on a wooden bench of the kind typically found in old-fashioned railway stations. I was tired and hungry, but so desperate was I fearing that an M.P. might be prowling this out-of-the-way stopover, that I opted for primly sitting up on the hard bench in as dignified a pose as I could muster. Oh, Mother, could you but see me now! Some of that lady-like stuff you tried so hard to teach me must have rubbed off.

The next day, the return to my barracks was accomplished with no further mishaps. My relief was short-lived. My friends greeted me in hushed and worried tones. "Boy, are you in trouble!" "They've been looking all over for you." "You'd better go straight to the Chief Nurse."

The Chief Nurse was furious and disgusted. Under other circumstances, I might have thought she was motherly with her cloud of white hair piled high and her ample bosom, but she was anything but benign when she confronted me. Was she thinking, "Here stands the miscreant before me. What have I done to deserve this ignorant, young truant and all the other young things like her who are bent on giving me more white hairs and ruining the good name of the corps"? And to me she railed, "Didn't you know you were AWOL? How could you have been so stupid?" Looking at me standing mute before her, she probably concluded that I wasn't worth making a federal case over. With disdain, she waved me out of her office. I hadn't endeared myself to her. I hadn't meant to ruin her day. But, all in all, I thought it went rather well.

An indelible imprint on my psyche resulted from an incident in the mess-hall. Several nurses who had returned from overseas tours came in. We, or others like us, were to be their replacements. They were being relieved of duty because of extreme fatigue having been through the worst of it for a long, long time. They were in their dress uniforms; they were straight and dignified. There was no frivolity to celebrate their homecoming. Their faces were inscrutable except for their eyes. Their eyes told the story of what they had been through. I sat in awe of them. Seeing them gave me a greater sense of urgency to get "there", wherever that may be. I shall never forget them.

This next recollection of basic might be characterized as a memory best forgotten: At last! The day came when we got our first pass into town. We had been whipped into shape by then, a sparkling, cohesive group. We had purchased our dress uniforms along with our work clothes at the beginning of basic training. Except for my ill-fated train trip, I had not had the opportunity to be grand in my dress uniform. I got all dressed up, resplendent I thought, and sallied forth to take the town.

Oh, the thrill! Strutting down the streets of midtown Indianapolis! At some distance away I spied a captain approaching. I measured his steps and mine. I was going to flash him the snappiest salute he ever had. I waited until he was at precisely the right diagonal from me to flash my salute.....and fell off the curb and sprawled in the street. Well, nature has a way of banishing pain, and to this day, I cannot tell you what happened next. Humiliation, thy name is a sassy young lieutenant.

One day in town, a group of us basics had an unpleasant experience involving a group of Wacs which colored my appraisal of them for awhile. This particular time, a group of them strung themselves, several abreast, across the width of the sidewalk. If we gave way to them, we were forced off the curb. If we had a confrontation, we could have forced them, by pulling rank, to salute us. None of us had the stomach for that kind of unpleasantness. A little inservice rivalry, notwithstanding, my rapport with them suffered until I met a dedicated woman who helped me immeasurably at my next duty station.

March 31, 1945. Basic training culminated with a full dress review and a diploma. We were anxious to see where we were to be posted. We had grown close during the rigors of our month of basic, but our excitement of looking forward to our first real assignment was blunted by the knowledge that we would be dispersed to several hospital facilities. My orders came. I would be going to Newton D. Baker Army Hospital, Martinsburg, West Virginia. My heart sank when I learned that Clenie would be sent to Nichols General in Louisville, Kentucky, but my spirits rose almost immediately when I discovered that Schmitty would be going with me.

In a transient environment such as the armed services, one grabs for security and comfort through friendships, temporary though most are. If one is fortunate enough to have a buddy of long duration, it's like taking a piece of home along on your journey. Schmitty was that kind of security.

*I had not had the opportunity to be grand in my dress
uniform. I got all dressed up, resplendent I thought, and
sallied forth to take the town.*

Billings General Hospital

Fort Benjamin Harrison

2d Lt Meredith J. Miller, N768837, AUS (ANC)

having completed the course in basic training

for the Reserve Army Nurse

Corps merits this

Diploma

in witness thereof the affixed signatures.

31 March 1945

Commanding
Wm. C. POLLOCK, Colonel, M.C.

Principal Chief Nurse
ANNA G. ANDERSON, Major, A.N.C.

Basic training culminated with a full dress review and a diploma

Newton D. Baker

I had left basic training, if not under a cloud, at least not as a favorite daughter. After my inadvertent AWOL episode, nothing I did escaped the watchful eye of the Chief Nurse. Her disenchantment with me increased in increments proportional to her irritation.

Our instructions for departing the base had been to place our gear on the curb outside our barracks where trucks would retrieve our belongings and transfer them to trains, each of which, hopefully, corresponded to the owners' destinations.

I was late getting my gear out to the curb for pickup. The white-haired nurse came into the barracks and heatedly berated me for being so slow. Now, I'm very methodical, and on this occasion, as was my wont, I was packing carefully. With my chief's bosom heaving, and the veins standing out on her neck, I decided that I was bad for her well-being and began tossing things in scoops and wads into my val-pak and duffel bag. I know she must have looked to the Heavens and prayed that she be spared another like me.

Thirty nurses entrained for Newton D. Baker. Privately, each one pondered what was in store at our first real duty station.

We arrived in Martinsburg early on Easter morning, April 1, 1945. We trudged up a hill ascending from the railroad tracks to a church that beckoned to us. There we attended services on a beautiful Easter morning. It was so peaceful there that, for awhile, we did not dwell on any grim duty that awaited us, that of caring for the cream of our manhood, now crippled and maimed.

Newton D. Baker General Hospital was fashioned similar to the others that had been constructed in anticipation of an influx of wounded. Narrow, one-story buildings were connected by a continuous corridor that passed at right angles through the middle of each building, continuing outside for several feet to the next building and so on. Each narrow building was a ward. Construction was begun on March 17, 1943 and completed on January 9, 1944, so the hospital was a little over a year old when my comrades and I took up our duties there.

The hospital was named in honor of Newton Diehl Baker, the United States Secretary of War in 1917 and 1918 during World War I. Mr. Baker was mayor of Cleveland, Ohio, was appointed to the Court of International Justice at the Hague, and received a medal from the National Institute of Social Services for service to humanity. He was a native of Martinsburg, West Virginia.

We had not been expected until the next day, Monday, April 2, but we were given our assignments immediately and would report to our respective wards at 0700 the next morning.

After a busy day getting oriented to our new surroundings, I finally was ensconced in my new quarters. It was then that it struck me. Ohmygosh! I don't have any luggage! Any clothes! There must have been a certain irony in that, but it eluded me at the moment. I was still in my dress uniform. I had carried a khaki, canvas musette bag on the train, but all it contained was a change of underwear, my tooth brush and some makeup. Alas, no duty uniform and cap. Poor Schmitty. It wouldn't be the first time that she had come to my rescue. She lent me one of her uniforms so that I could go on duty in the morning. It would not have been prudent of me to get off on the wrong foot with this new chief nurse.

Our ward duty uniforms were singularly unglamorous. They were brown and white pin stripe, seersucker wrap-arounds not unlike the Hoover[7] aprons of the 30's. They conjured up the image of housewives in their Hoover wrap-arounds and their white ankle socks and sandals, hanging out the wash. Our seersuckers were topped with a strange seersucker cap. There are those who fall in love with anything in uniform but decidedly not the aforementioned. However, I did think our dress uniforms were pretty "snazzy". I hadn't joined the army to be glamorous, but I still wear my uniform with pride whenever I am asked to speak and requested to come in uniform. I confess I am not as svelte as I was those many years ago, but still, being able to don it pleases me. I still own my brown, leather oxfords. They were standard issue for both dress and stateside duty. They carried me many, many miles and have yet to show any wear. (In fact, my daughter, who thought they were "cool", wore them all through college.) We had in our shoe wardrobe a "clunky", ankle-high boot with a thick sole, a broad heel and a bulbous hard toe. They were so ugly that we dubbed them "corrective shoes for crippled children". By far, my favorite foot-wear were my combat boots that I lived in overseas.

Many tracers were sent to track my gear, and they yielded nothing. I had lost everything including many personal items. It took several trips to nearby Baltimore and much expense to get re-outfitted.

Schmitty and I had twin assignments in the paraplegic wards. It was hard duty and emotionally draining. There were so many of them. Several of their wives, unable to face the future without a family or lacking the steadfastness to deliver long-term care, were divorcing their husbands. Additionally, to the obvious physical handicaps that necessitated artificially clearing nonfunctioning bowels and bladder, they were universally depressed. If there were some way to buoy their spirits, to maybe get a little smile........

Schmitty and I were in complete accord, and we had a plan. At 0700 we would stand outside the doors of the ward, steeling our resolve to face what was on the other side. She would say, "Are you ready?", and I would answer, "Yep! I'm ready!" whereupon we would fling open the doors and go into our "song and dance". I don't know which one of us was the straight man, but we tossed a continuous line of outrageous patter. There weren't any talent scouts around, but our act rivaled that of a well-known, modern day sit-com, "Laverne and Shirley"[8]. Some of our boys would smile. Some even laughed. They got so that they waited expectantly for us to fling open those doors.

A few of our patients were strong enough to be in wheelchairs. They took full advantage of their mobility as they went hot-rodding up and down the wards, careening around the beds, doing "wheelies" as they made a circle spin at the end of the ward, then tearing up the center aisle to the opposite end.

They were a hazard to life and limb, but one wheelchair "jock" put my dignity in peril. I was standing at the bedside bathing one of my patients. Drag-racing with his wheelchair, this obvious mischief-maker zoomed up to the bed, and with deadly accuracy, flung a dead mouse at me. I am ashamed to say that I reacted in typical female fashion, squealing and jumping on something high, in this case the bed with my arms encircling my startled patient's neck. Immediately, I tried to regain my composure (and dignity) , but too late. The ward was in convulsions at my plight. But wasn't it wonderful to hear them laugh?

I was transferred to night duty, still with my fellas on the paraplegic ward. The night shift was twelve hours from 7:00(1900) PM. to 7:00(0700) AM. It seemed that I spent the entire night preparing penicillin syringes, administering them and starting all over again. All the paraplegics received penicillin every three hours day and night. The long-lasting form had not been developed at this time. In fact, penicillin was so new that my experience with it in civilian hospitals as a student nurse was very rare. Civilian hospitals could obtain it in limited quantities for critically ill patients at a prohibitive cost. All the rest went to the military.

Streptomycin was the next antibiotic to appear following soon after the introduction of penicillin. It, too, went almost exclusively to the military.

Sometimes I thought all the penicillin was on the paraplegic wards. With my cafeteria tray full of rows of syringes, each sterile needle resting on its alcohol sponge, I would make my every-three-hour excursion up and down the ward "shooting" my sleeping patients. Since my lads had no sensation in their lower body, most generally, I could lift the covers, and wing in a shot without disturbing their sleep. This procedure was not always feasible with the newly admitted patients.

Those recently wounded were still suffering from varying degrees of shellshock[9] and were extremely agitated. No matter how stealthily I approached them, they reacted violently to the slightest movement with outcries and flailing arms, usually connecting with a blow on me and shattering the syringe. When they were fully awake, they would be contrite and apologetic for having hit their nurse.

It was often difficult for me to face rows of
cots filled with the wounded and helpless. And I remember the young heads cradled on hospital pillows with faces smooth of cheek and with stricken eyes. From where I sit now, looking at fifty year old photographs of young soldiers with their smooth skin and remnants of baby fat, I know they were just boys.

My older son dropped out of college to take his chance on the Vietnam draft. Even though the quota was filled before his number was called, I, nevertheless, experienced the dark, sickening fear deep in my gut that every mother, through the ages, has felt.

My next assignment was the plastic surgery ward. It was not my business to question changes of assignments. Perhaps a pattern of rotation was practiced so that one's spirit didn't get submerged in the sadness of any one ward or patient. Or perhaps it prevented a patient from getting too attached to his nurse. In this case, I was secretly relieved to get a respite from the paraplegic wards. However, the plastic surgery wards did not yield the anticipated relief.

I will not go into the technology of the complicated operations involved in plastic surgery whereby tissue was transferred in lengthy stages from one part of the body to another, and yet another, as many times as it took for that tissue to reach the area where it was going to be used. Suffice to say, miracles were wrought. Jaws, lips, eyebrows, temples, cheeks, ears, noses, all rebuilt by a tedious course of tissue transfer, the tissue being molded on a base of grafted bone.

One of my boys was a tanker. He was eighteen. He had escaped the inferno of his burning tank, but he was hideously, grotesquely disfigured. He kept a '"before" picture by his bed to remind us that what we saw was not really he, that the shell he carried now merely concealed the self within. In his picture, he was unbelievably handsome.

At the time he became my patient, the doctors were trying to give him workable hands before they started on his face. Webs of scar tissue had to be carved away from his fingers, tendons stretched, skin grafted over the whole of his hands, backs and palms. He was in for many years of treatment. I was to see him again after the war.

In later years, I was to wonder whether any of the tankers whom I tended were from my husband's armored division. It would be a long while before our lives converged, but could fate have put me in proximity with anyone who had been close to him?

While I will not detail too many patients and procedures, it is pertinent to give some examples. This is what I did. It was my job. I could scarcely tell a story about an army nurse without telling about her work, so between adventures, there was serious business going on. With that caution, I will tell about one of my boys, the memory of whom I will take to my grave. It is difficult to pen this, impossible to talk about out loud. In talking to groups, I have never been able to get through this part: He had no face. He had eyes and a larynx - and nothing in between. Every morning, it fell to me to clean his - well, where his face had been. I couldn't eat breakfast those mornings. I had made him laugh and so, he was always in the treatment room at 0700 sharp, my first patient of the day. With my back to him, I busied myself at the dressing cart, squeezing my eyes tight so the tears wouldn't spill out and gulping back gags as best I could. I fought for composure. When, finally, I turned to him, instruments in hand, I told him every outrageous joke I could think of as I cleaned the oozing, formless, viscous mass. The chortling that emanated from his larynx told me that I had made him laugh, if just for a minute. It was my jokes and the respect and dignity with which I cared for him that brought him to me the first of the day. I prayed that not so much as a flicker in my demeanor would betray how much his plight hurt me. Dear God, to this day, the anguish has not abated.

There was a rule that lady officers did not fraternize with the enlisted men, socially. I had never been able to completely subvert the rebel that still burned inside me, so when a good-looking young corpsman asked me out, I accepted. My contrary inner voice was rationalizing that I reserved the right to choose my own friends, and that it would be the height of snobbery to hold my officer status over him - besides, he had a car.

The end of the evening was a calamity, so much so that I do not remember if I had any fun at the beginning of my big date. He parked the car, and without further ceremony, tried to take liberties with me. I had run into "leches" before, but not many because, for the most part, Mother's admonition that if "I behave like a lady, I will be treated like a lady" had proved true. Disappointment is too mild when I questioned how this comely youth could be so ugly? I learned from ward scuttlebutt that his modus operandi was to date, and if possible, bed as many nurses as he could. He must have harbored terrible resentment against working under lady officers that he needed to debase them to charge his sagging ego.

The end result of my lapse in obeying the rules was that this corpsman never cooperated with me again in performing his ward duties. It was a form of psychological blackmail knowing that if I put him on report, he could shine the light on my own complicity. I do not know if he cooperated with the ones who had succumbed to his seduction, but, as for me, it was an unwelcome learning experience.

> This is a propitious time to explain how I modified my preadolescent vows of never marrying or never having babies. I still felt that both possibilities were remote, but I left the door ajar. On the teensiest, weensiest, most infinitesimal chance that I would one day marry, I was going into that union brand new. And on the teensiest, weensiest, most infinitesimal chance that I would have a family, my babies were going to be born free of any taint. Would my goals be laughable now? I still think they were worthy challenges. The more battles I had in the back of a "recon" car, the more stubborn became my resolve.

Our days at Newton D. Baker were so compacted that it seemed as if we were stationed there longer than sixty-eight calendar days. My quarters there were the nicest I was to have for the rest of my tenure. We were lodged in attractive, well-appointed two bed rooms. Initially, I shared the room with another nurse, but she was transferred, leaving me to luxuriate by myself. Such privacy was rare.

Newton D. Baker was also prison to a large compound of German internees. It was not seemly for us to detour around the compound to satisfy our curiosity about them, and we were forbidden to do so. It disturbed me to see female relatives of the patients standing outside the metal enclosure, gawking at them. The prisoners, pressed against the fence gaping at the onlookers, were a silent and sullen bunch. The whole thing had a zoo-like quality. I dare say that, in our prisons, they were well-fed and well-cared for, unlike the fate of our men in German and Japanese prisons. In retrospect, I am much more charitable toward the women whose sons, husbands, brothers were wounded by these Germans or others like them. In their own way, they had a need to confront their loved ones' enemy.

The difference in treatment between prisoners-of-war here and that of the German and Japanese prisons was heightened when I learned of the release from a German camp of a high-school beau. The Russians, on their drive west, freed the Americans when they came upon the camp. They could not stop their momentum to care for the prisoners. Instead, they told my friend and the others to make their way east, through Russia, and try to gain passage home from there, in his case, from Odessa on the Black Sea.

During his incarceration, I had joined the army. He had much catching up to do and coming to see me was part of the normalizing process. It relieved me to note his progress toward robust health, and it was on that visit that he divulged a little of what he had endured. The present direction of my life was inalterably cemented in. It was goodbye to one who had already put his future on hold to serve his country. And I was just beginning.

The prisoners had daily work detail, and I often would see them buffing the wooden corridors with large polishing machines. I was coming off night duty at 0730. I was tired and looking forward to snuggling down in my bed. My roommate was gone, and I knew I would be undisturbed. Hurrying, I burst through the door. The abruptness with which I halted almost toppled me. I had walked in on a startling scene. There in my room, one on each bed, were two German prisoners, goofing off from their work detail. They had picked my room to have their smoke break. The guard for the work crew was not in evidence. It was too creepy for me. I wheeled out of the room and spent my time in the reception lounge until, finally, I could go to bed. Older and more assertive now, I might have handled the situation differently. Then, I only wanted to put distance between us.

And it was at Newton D. Baker, on April 12, 1945, that I learned of the death of our Commander-In-Chief, Franklin Delano Roosevelt. I had not matured enough to include politics in my repertoire of interests, but I was aware of the devastation to my countrymen of this sobering news. In the middle of a war, we had lost our leader.

Nothing remains static, and the next disruption to our routine was a new overseas quota to be met. Our chief nurse probably thought her hospital was a revolving door with her new nurses going out with unnerving rapidity. She preferred to fill her quotas with the older girls, and she regarded her last group entirely too young. Both Schmitty and I had put our names on the overseas list, and then we proceeded to nag our chief to let us go. She either could not fill her quota without us, or we had worn her down. We had made the list.

We left Newton D. Baker for our one and only furlough, the obligatory overseas leave.

My trench coat and I became fast friends

Our ward duty uniforms were singularly unglamorous.

One of my boys was a tanker. He was grotesquely disfigured from burns. This is his "before" picture.

The Troop Train

I had fifteen days to neatly tuck away my memories of home to take on my journey. I do not recall feeling sad or nostalgic, only rueful about how all this was affecting my family. I was too curious to see what was around the next bend to succumb to doubts about the future. My parents were over-extending themselves to show me a good time with picnics and parties and lots of picture taking. My little brother, now eleven, wanted me visible and in uniform so he could show me off. Father wanted to corral me for serious talks in his study. He felt an urgency to dispense every piece of fatherly advice at his disposal lest this be the last chance he could perform his parental duties.

Father had long been convinced that everything I did conspired to unhinge him. I could not persuade him that I was not a mutinous child plotting to defy him. He had assumed his husband and father duties unfalteringly, and those duties included holding and protecting his girl children close in the bosom of the family. His middle child troubled him deeply. She simply would not conform, and now she was going off to heavens knows where. Earnestly, he had told me to be sure to go to Europe. Further, I should not consider the Pacific Theatre because there were too many diseases in that corner of the world. Poor Father, for the first time, he was defeated. He had always called the shots, and he saw the grip he had had on the fate of his family slipping away. I reminded him that I was my father's daughter. It was he who taught me to think independently; to be stalwart, resolute and disciplined; to surround myself with good books and good music; to be ethical in the market place in all my dealings; to be fair and just and compassionate; and finally, to be true to myself. It was this last dictum that I was playing out with the course of action I had chosen, and it was this that Father could not accept.

It was back to Newton D. Baker after our leave to await orders for the next leg of our journey. On June 9, 1945, we boarded a train for the west coast. Yes, it was to be the Pacific

Theatre. For a minute, there flashed a picture of Father's consternation when he would learn of our destination.

With a group of thirty departing Newton D. Baker, we filled one coach. One of our girls had a tendency for getting drunk at any stressful life event. I wondered how she would handle an emergency in the field. She was consistent, however. I'll give her that. It was late at night when we boarded the train at Martinsburg, and sure enough, three girls were "pouring" her onto the train. She had the night to sleep it off before she met her father at a lay-over in Chicago.

Our coach was to be our home for several days. It was tormenting for Schmitty and me when our route took us through Akron. Schmitty and I watched as the train rolled through our town, now dark and asleep, desolate at not being able to stop and call our parents.

In Chicago, we were shunted off on a siding, there to spend the night. We awoke in the stock yards. That seemed appropriate. Many times I felt that we were so much livestock being prodded aboard trucks, planes and trains with no knowledge of our fate.

Our coach was hot and dirty by day and freezing at night. The train was heading southwest, and it seemed, by some capricious design, that we traveled through the valleys and desert in the heat of the day and through the chill of the mountains at night. Every available coach, freight car, vehicle, plane or ship had been pressed into service for war transportation. This coach looked like a relic whose glory days were long past, and now, like "The Little Engine That Could"[10], with new pride, it was carrying nurses to their appointment with destiny.

We had our own porter assigned to us who made up our berths every night. I shared an upper with Schmitty. Now, Schmitty was tall and angular with no spare fat to keep her warm. As we huddled together for a modicum of warmth under one threadbare blanket, her shivering bones played a tattoo on me. I was sure I would be permanently bruised.

At some point, we were hitched on the end of a long troop train. Up to that time, we had been orphans being shunted onto a siding any time something more urgent came along.

Three times a day, we took our mess gear and ran a gauntlet through several cars of G.I.s to the mess car in the front of the train. If the train swayed and we lost our balance falling against one of the soldiers, the cheers and whistles filled the train. It was innocent sport, but it made our three-times-daily trek the full length of the train and back a marathon event.

Our ride on a troop train was tedious, but it was on that trip that I met some of the nicest faces in America. At every hamlet and burg where the train stopped, the townspeople were waiting by the tracks with coffee, sandwiches, and homebaked goodies.

California, Here I Come

Our destination was Camp Beale, California. All of us, who had been dispersed to different hospitals after basic training, converged here. This camp would be an extension of basic training emphasizing skills we would need for overseas duty. These included map reading, gas mask drills, abandon ship drills and marching with full equipment.

Here, I saw my first black troops. Growing up in a segregated society, I was not even aware of segregation. My contact with black people was limited to the crew who collected the ashes from the coal furnace and to Hester who helped my mother.

My sister and I loved Hester. We would wait at the bus stop at the corner. When the bus sputtered to a stop belching black smoke out its hind end, we would hold our breath with eager anticipation until it disengorged Hester. Upon espying her, we would grab her and hug her so enthuiasitically, we would send her hat askew and cause her to lose her balance. Hester was a little bitty thing. After righting her hat to its prim angle and smoothing her dress, she would trudge up the street with two strapping youngsters hanging on her arms.

On the occasion that I would be left alone, Mother would always caution me never to open the door to anyone. Upon her return, she would check to see if I had obeyed her order. I remember being so proud when I told her that I hadn't let anyone in except the ash man and his crew.

The two incidents above were the sum total of my experience with another race, both positive experiences. So, when I saw the black platoons marching down the streets, I was entranced. And when they sang as they marched in a collective, deep, throaty baritone, it was electrifying.

Our platoon marched too - everywhere. We sang, too, the typical "Sound Off":

> "They say that in the army,
>   The food is mighty fine.
>   A roll fell off the table
>   And killed a pal of mine."
> Refrain: "Oh, I don't want no
>   more of army life,
>   I just wanta go,
>   I just wanta go,
>   I just wanta go home."..ad infinitum.

We also bellowed a rowdy rendition of:
 " The First Lieutenants are winning the war, parlez vous!
 The First Lieutenants are winning the war, parlez vous!
 The First Lieutenants are winning the war,
 So what in the Hell are we fighting for?
 Inky dinky, parlez vous."

We cut a pretty mean swath ourselves marching in our fatigues, helmits, gas masks and packs.

The gas mask drills involved going into a little shed that had been flooded with gas. Upon entering, we were to hold our breath as we pulled the mask from its case; secured it properly on our face; blew through the mask and canister to clear it of any gas, and then it was safe to breathe through the mask. No cheating like loosening the fasteners of the mask case ahead of time. Fumble fingers would not work in this exercise.

I developed a phobia, a fear of heights, at some point in my life, but it had not made its appearance at the time we would be practicing abandon ship drills. In fact, I was exhilarated with every phase of our training. In this exercise, cargo nets were slung from the side of a mock-up of a ship. The drill involved scaling the net, making your body a small silhouette as you hugged the top rail and clambering down the other side. Some of the girls froze on the net, and the men conducting the drill had to carry them down. I called them pansies. I recant that epithet now in view of my own height fear.

For me, map reading was an oxymoron. I have no spatial awareness. I can get lost coming out of a shopping mall, so it was with a certain amount of self-derision that I undertook the map reading course. I understood the principles. Intellectually, they made perfect sense to me. It was simply that out in the field, I had no sense of direction even when employing the principles. My leaving for overseas duty was contingent on my passing the map course. Miraculously, I made it, but my passing was akin to memorizing theorems for math class, taking the test and promptly forgetting the whole miserable thing.

We wore our bulbous-toed ankle boots in the field and for marching, but my dress oxfords got a workout at Camp Beale walking to and from the officers' club. It was three miles to the officers' club from our barracks. Often, I would have an early morning breakfast date, and just as often, a supper date. The officers' club was another kind of training ground. We were all transplants from our home environment. We were all dressed in the same olive drab. Choosing friends was a judgment call.

It was difficult for a non-drinker to get into a convivial mood. I wanted to be part of the merriment without imbibing to get there. So many at the club seemed to have an "eat, drink, and be merry for tomorrow we die" philosophy. Such a state of mind is not uncommon in wartime.

> Picturing the whole scenario now reminds me of a pervasive attitude that existed at the height of the cold war. How we coped is illustrated by an example that concerns my oldest son: He had come into my room at midnight after a date, and he had said, "Mom, how do you live your life and plan for the future with the threat of nuclear war influencing everything you do?" He had thrown his mother a terrible curve. I had pondered that question myself. Did I have the wisdom to give him what he sought? And, I thought, "How do I live my life?" I realized that I plant my flowers every spring. I plan for tomorrow, next week and next year. And I said to him that you have to live each day as if there is going to be a tomorrow. You cannot do something today that is alien to your nature, and then, wake up and find that tomorrow is here, and you've blown it. If there were to be no tomorrow, you would be "beyond

the pale" and regrets would be nonexistent. And, I still plant my flowers every spring.

Maybe it was because I didn't drink. Maybe I didn't look very intimidating. Maybe I looked vulnerable. At any rate, I seemed to attract what I called "protectors", men who took it upon themselves to shield me from some of the harsher aspects of army life. That brand of chivalry is scarce in the context of today's society. I rather liked it. They were sweet and kind, and I shall be forever grateful for their interest in me. We dined and danced in the nicest places in nearby Sacramento. I don't think I missed a thing.

Camp Beale was barren, flat, treeless and hot. It was with few regrets that we bade farewell and headed for what was to be our point of embarkation.

This page is copied from the original flag
that hung in the window at my home

The government was talking about drafting nurses. This is one of many examples of advertising that appeared in magazines in the 1940's.

CHAPEL AND GUEST HOUSE, NEWTON D. BAKER GENERAL HOSPITAL, MARTINSBURG, W. VA.

ADMINISTRATION BUILDING, NEWTON D. BAKER GENERAL HOSPITAL, MARTINSBURG, W. VA.

Newton D. Baker General Hospital in Martinsburg, West Virgina.

*We were on our way on the U.S.S. Marigold, a somewhat decrepit old lady
who wasn't too fussy about her grooming.*

Point of Embarkation

We were on a sleeper headed for Camp Anza located near Riverside, California.The camp had no special facilities for women. At the very least in dormitory and barracks situations, we were accustomed to shower stalls and toilets in cubicles. It was incumbent on us to adapt to communal showers and latrines.

I was very modest. Most of us were. I was also inhibited. I had always felt that one's inhibitions served as a sort of science fiction "force field", its purpose being to protect the innocent and inexperienced from emotional activities beyond one's capabilities to handle them. As we progress through our lifespan, it seems to me that we reach the different phases of our growth at the proper time. So it was, with my inhibitions intact, I took one look at the shower room and decided I would take sponge baths for the duration of my stay there. Admitting that my physiology was identical to other females, I, none-the-less, cherished my privacy and, at least, pretended that I was doing it my way.

We still did not know our destination, but it was going to be hot. We were instructed to send all our woolens home, and were issued sun-tans. These were cotton twill long-sleeved shirts and slacks. We got two pairs of combat boots, and we began packing our foot-lockers. They would go into the hold of the ship. For me, that was like burying mine alive for the rest of the war.

I was in a panic about being in some primitive place with a scarcity of equipment for female hygiene. With that in mind, and with a goodly investment, I lined the bottom of my foot-locker, three layers deep, with sanitary pads and layered my underwear and other gear on top. By golly! I wasn't going to be caught short! Well, my theory was great. But, in actual practice, it stunk. My foot-locker never caught up with me. Once overseas, I moved every two to six weeks, and by the time my foot-locker caught up with my last duty station, I had moved on.

To make matters worse, my internal time clock was subject to the vagaries of my erratic schedule. I was in need of the contents of my errant foot-locker every time I moved, and every time I moved, I could be found roaring down the road as the truck was pulling out with my compatriots hanging over the tailgate yelling, "Come on, Miller! Come on, Miller!". I would heave my gear over the tailgate, and they would reel me in. I assumed that these episodes triggered my time clock. As for my lack of punctuality, I had not shown much improvement since basic training. In reference to my deprivation of equipment, the army thinks of everything.

Preparations and instructions proceeded. We were told we would be part of a convoy sailing under blackout conditions. We were not permitted to call our parents or to divulge details of our departure to anyone. One girl, Mary Kay, lost her father and was not allowed to go East to attend his funeral. The camp commander summoned Schmitty, another girl and me and told us to take her into Los Angeles and get her drunk. While I was not in agreement with his prescription, I jumped at the chance to see Los Angeles.

We felt we were among the chosen to get a pass into town, but as the bus rumbled toward Los Angeles, the slogan, "Loose lips, sink ships" played like a broken record in my mind. It was one of several reminders that spies lurked everywhere. The most casual contact or careless word could jeopardize a troop movement or a convoy. So earnest was I about keeping my lips buttoned that I scarcely talked lest I blurt out something provocative to "the spies all around me." By shouldering the burden of secrecy, I thought that I had assured a safe crossing for the convoy. As for Mary Kay, she got very drunk that night without our encouragement.

The numbers on the calendar flipped by fast. Deep in our solar plexus was a mixture of excitement and apprehension. The camp commander called us together the night before our departure with disturbing news. We would not sail with the protection of a convoy after all. We would make our crossing, alone, on a hospital ship with all its lights ablaze like a new saloon. According to the Geneva Convention, a hospital ship cannot be attacked. The huge red cross on the stack always would be illuminated so there would be no mistake. However, the Japanese were never known to concern themselves with the Geneva Convention. The commander further announced that the Japanese had attacked one of our hospital ships; we had retaliated, and now, it was their turn again. (Historically, I have no knowledge of an attack by our forces on an enemy hospital ship. I am assuming it may have been a transport that coincidentally carried wounded.) A sister ship, the U.S.S. Comfort was struck by a Japanese suicide plane on April 29, 1945 while evacuating wounded from Okinawa to Guam. Twenty-eight, including six nurses, were killed and forty-eight others were wounded.

The hospital ship, the U.S.S. Newfoundland,
was bombed and sunk in the Tyrrenian Sea off the
coast of Salerno, Italy on September 13, 1943.

We felt like a sentence had been pronounced. We were told to get on the 'phone, call our parents, tell them all the details of our voyage. The Japanese already knew so why shouldn't our parents?

The next morning, we shouldered our gear and embarked on the U.S.S. Marigold from the port of San Pedro, California.

THE CROSSING

We were on our way in a somewhat decrepit old lady who had been converted into a hospital ship. In the midst of the throng wending its way up the gangway, a voice piped up with the civilian gas rationing slogan, "Is this trip necessary?"

The U.S.S. Marigold would be our home for the next twenty-nine days. She was one of four hospital ships named after flowers. There were the Larkspur, the Wisteria, the Dogwood and ours. These converted ships had been freighters or troop transports. The Larkspur was the oldest, having been built in Germany in 1901. She served in Europe. The Marigold, built in New Jersey in 1920, was the ex-President Fillmore.

The minute I stepped aboard, I knew she was old and not too fussy about her grooming. This was not going to be a luxury cruise. It was hot, dirty, cramped and uncomfortable. She was manned by a merchant marine crew, and while I do not wish to detract from the valuable service rendered by the Merchant Marine, this ship lacked the spit and polish of the navy ships.

There were six hundred nurses on board. We did not realize it then, but we were to be part of the invasion forces going into Japan.

As the ship pulled away, we were serenaded by an army band on the dock. It was playing "Sentimental Journey"[11], and as we put more distance between us and the dock, the sound still wafted across the water. The band players were scarcely visible now, but they were still playing "Sentimental Journey" over and over again. We did not make a sound, each one enveloped in her own cocoon of very private thoughts. I cannot verbalize how I felt at that moment. I can only say that I have hated "Sentimental Journey" ever since.

It was comforting to see the mail plane ply the skies back and forth for the first few days. We would see it as far as Hawaii when it, too, would desert us.

We occupied the bunks in the patient wards for our sleeping quarters. I was in an eighty bed ward. I was assigned to the top bunk of a four bunk tier. Huge heating or ventilating pipes criss-crossed the ceiling, one running directly over my bunk so close that it impinged upon my hip if I attempted to sleep on my side. We bathed in saltwater, "lathering" up with a special saltwater soap that did not lather. We were gritty from the soap and sticky from the saltwater. Our drinking water was at a premium and was always hot.

It was during one of our late night chats, when the heat and the growling engine noises coming from the bowels of the ship kept us awake, that we made our suicide pact. We vowed that if capture was imminent and rape was inevitable, we would kill ourselves. We hadn't figured out quite how we would accomplish this, but we were adamant in our resolve and confident that we could pull it off. It sounded like the kind of bravado one hears from green troops. Fortunately, we were not called upon to activate our pact.

In addition to the Merchant Marine crew, the ship was completely staffed by a permanent complement of army doctors and nurses who would go into action treating the wounded on the return trip. They had nice quarters on the top deck with a sun deck and other amenities. We saw them rarely, only when nurses came down to their wards and enlisted our help in some small duty. The rest of the time we were hard pressed to occupy our time. If one were seasick, one could languish in bed until it was all over, but I would not wish that on anybody.

Four hundred nurses disembarked at Hawaii. Those of us who remained sarcastically remarked, "Tough duty, that, Hawaii." Some fault of the ship cost a twenty-four hour layover for repairs. We were delighted. That meant shore leave. Schmitty and I thought we were going to do Honolulu. Instead, we wandered around aimlessly in the honky-tonk section of tattoo parlors and sleazy photographer shops designed to entice and exploit the servicemen. The seamy and carnival atmosphere caused us to hurry back to the ship early. It's funny how anything that harbored us became sanctuary, a barracks or a ship, homely though it was.

The next day, we were treated to a picnic on a lovely stretch of white beach. Real hula dancers performed, good-naturedly coaxing reluctant girls onto the sand to hula with them. It was fun. It was a welcome diversion because, though no one talked about it, our seriousness of purpose lay in the shallow waters of our consciousness. Credit goes to an unnamed service group for feting us. These groups did so much to alleviate both the boredom and the stress of the troops.

At this time, Hawaii had not undergone the postwar overbuilding with high-rise resort hotels spilling all over the beaches.

The tedium of the journey increased after we left Hawaii. The Pacific Ocean was like a millpond with the wake of our ship making the only ripples. It does not always present such a benign face, but where we were, fairly close to the equator, it looked harmless. And, it was hot! The sullen, motionless air, and the unrelenting sun rendered us listless and inert. I could imagine the torment of sailors becalmed, praying for a freshening of the winds. The forward motion of the ship stirred the air and offered some relief. Many girls spent part of the nights on deck to escape the stifling sleeping quarters. I would lie abed in my top bunk semi-stuporous, sleeping fitfully.

We tried to stay cooler by rolling up the sleeves and pant legs of our suntans. A superior officer thought that was offensive for officers to be so informal and told us to roll them back down and leave them that way.

Many played bridge all day. I had not learned the pastime so I availed myself of a library of tattered paperbacks. Sometimes, at night, I would drape myself over the deck rail and idly watch the phosphorus fire in the darkling water.

At one point, we were under surveillance by a submarine off our starboard side riding with periscope up. Since it was under no obligation to identify itself, we never learned whether it was theirs or ours. It stands to reason it was one of ours. Can you not imagine a crew of "dame" hungry submariners all taking their turn at the periscope to ogle the nurses lined up along the rail? The submarine rode along with us for some time, long enough for everyone inside to get a chance at the periscope.

Another time, we spent the daylight hours circling in ever widening concentric circles searching for survivors. We were never told what or for whom we were looking.

In otherwise desultory days, mealtimes were an event. Our numbers necessitated our eating in shifts. The small mess hall was furnished with long counters and permanently attached stools such as might be found in a diner. Each edge of the counters was capped with a molding to prevent our mess gear from careening off onto the floor if we hit some rough weather. We had been advised to eat every meal to allay seasickness. I had not shown any propensity toward that malady, and to keep it that way, I ate every meal.

There was a bit of squeamishness I would have to overcome were I to keep to my scheme of eating every meal. We were served cafeteria style from the galley. I can appreciate how difficult it was for the cooks to prepare three meals a day in the cramped, beastly hot galley. However, there was this massive tower of a man, in his soaked undershirt, standing in front of the galley serving window. His great belly bulged over the counter on which sat a huge kettle of stew, goulash or whatever. As we filed by, he would serve - make that plop - the concoction on our mess gear. The heat and his girth conspired to make him sweat profusely, and the sweat rolled down his face, his body, his arms and right into the kettle of food. And, wouldn't you know? It was he who stood there every single day dispensing the food, well flavored with the dubious added ingredient of his sweat. Hey! At least it was well salted.

Passengers, crew and complement of hospital personnel were all noncombatants, and as such, were not armed. It was no secret that the crew carried well concealed side arms, albeit they were illegal arms.

The crew was very much in evidence, mingling, fraternizing and more. Despite our solemn intent, we were possessed of human frailties, and some of the girls, lonely for attention and flattered by the men, succumbed to their seductive blandishments. Several decks below in the ship were locked cages with bunks in them which housed the psychiatric patients from the war zones. The miracle of chemotherapy to treat psychoses was not available then, and though it may sound inhumane, locked cages protected them from running amok and jumping overboard. It was to these cages that the girls were lured, a perfect hideaway for their dalliances.

The upshot of these young women being compromised by the crew was that three girls were taken off the ship with gonorrhea, and two collapsed with nervous breakdowns. From general observation, it seemed that the girls with the breakdowns appeared to be the most vulnerable and the most incapable of handling an emotional catastrophe.

I wanted to investigate the psychiatric wards too, and when a young crew member offered to show me the way, I accepted. I almost became a victim when it became obvious he had other things on his agenda besides a tour of the wards. I talked my way out of that one, but I was ashamed that I had been so gullible.

In addition to Schmitty and Clenie, I met Janie. Janie was older than the rest of us. She was thirty-five. She had enlisted in the army as a prescription to help turn her life around after a painful divorce. She became my dear friend for the rest of her life.

Janie and Clenie both became ill with a flu-like illness and were confined to sick bay along with the aforementioned girls. Our journey was nearing completion. Like sailors of yore, eagerly searching for the first shadow on the horizon and, at last, singing out, "Land ho!", we, too, sought the first glimpse of land. We were rewarded with our first sighting of the Philippines. We dropped anchor at the island of the Leyte.

It soon became apparent why we had detoured to Leyte. The captain was anxious to rid his ship of its patients. It seems he could not wait until we reached Manila Bay in Luzon which offered better medical facilities. Leyte lay on the eastern edge of the Philippine Archipelago. We had arrived there first, and the captain could "cleanse" his ship a few days sooner. It was as if it were a banishment.

A narrow ladder was slung at a steep angle along the side of the ship. The ambulatory girls descended first to a waiting barge. There was no derision, only silence, when the two Section 8's, the army's medical designation for mental illness, came down the ladder, whimpering and jibbering. It was a pitiful, heartbreaking cap to their army career.

Janie's stretcher made it down the ladder without incident. Then the men, one on each end of Clenie's stretcher, began their descent. Clenie lay there with all her gear piled on her abdomen. Watching from above, we were shouting words of encouragement to her. Suddenly, there was a unison scream as we saw Clenie's stretcher tipping dangerously toward the perpendicular. We watched, horrified, as Clenie, gear and all, began sliding toward the sea. There was a frantic struggle as the men fought to right the stretcher and get a grip on Clenie, the effort almost toppling all of them into the ocean. The whole scene was beginning to look like a burial at sea.

We were underway again. I was subdued, thinking with concern about the recently departed girls. And, yes, feeling abandoned without Clenie and Janie.

Soon, we would put into Manila Bay, the scene of fierce battles; of names like Bataan and Corregidor; of prayers for captured nurses who had been interned in Japanese prisons for three years.

I was ready for the next chapter.

THE PHILIPPINES

Manila Bay

We dropped anchor far from shore. Manila Bay was so cluttered with dead ships, both submerged and partially submerged, as to make navigation impossible. Eager as we were to leave the ship and feel land under our feet, we were to be detained on board for another twenty-four hours.

The ennui of that last day and night was mitigated by a surprise visit of some officers whom we had met at Camp Beale. The army grapevine far outstripped jungle drums because they were making arrangements for a barge at the first appearance of our ship in the bay. They could not stay on board and we could not leave, but just their being there made our arrival more auspicious. I wonder if they had any inkling that their impulse to ride out to the Marigold was such a welcome gesture?

By now, most of us were turning a putrid yellow, sort of jaundice-chic. About two weeks before journey's end, we were started on the anti-malarial drug, Atabrine. It not only turned one's skin yellow, but one's perspiration took on a bilious hue.

I was never too fond of yellow and red in combination, but, in our case, it became very "in" to have a slash of lip scarlet leaping out from a yellow background. "Vogue"[12] never picked up on it though.

We were packed, on deck and ready when the barges came alongside at dawn. Although the water was not too angry, the undulating sea created swells and troughs with the ship and the barge, each in its turn, riding high on the crest of the wave or plunging deep into the trough. Loaded with our gear, we descended the ladder, poised to leap into the barge at the precise moment the barge heaved up out of the trough as the ship was coming down from the height of the swell. When each vessel was on a relatively even plane to each other, as they were trading places from trough to swell, we leaped. The barges, LCI's (Landing Craft Infantry), were of the kind one sees in the invasion movies. The high straight sides obscured our vision so we did not have to watch as the barge threaded its way through the graveyard of ships.

Presently, the front panel dropped down, and we "invaded" the Philippines and headed for an uncertain future.

Novaliches

We had scarcely hit the beach when we were herded into trucks, and all too soon, were plunging through the jungle. If any of us had entertained the idea that we would stay in Manila, bombed out though it was, we were mistaken. We never knew where we were going. From some higher echelon came the barges, the trucks, the planes and the food and cots. Each of us in the service had his or her own job to do, but none of us concerned ourselves with the mundane considerations of food and shelter. That was someone else's job. That is not to imply that Americans were not capable of independent thought. In both the Pacific and European Theaters, the war was won, in part, because our military could step in to fill the breech caused by the loss of a superior. Americans were not rendered militarily impotent if their leaders were killed.

Finally, when we had come to a clearing, we caught our first glimpse of Novaliches, an abandoned Jesuit monastery. It was to be our home while we waited for assignments.

A hospital, with a full roster of personnel, went overseas as a complete entity. Its members had a bond with each other, and an identification with their unit that they would carry with them the rest of their lives. We had no such bond. Individually, we had a paper assignment to one of these existing units. We were to be replacements for those relieved of duty, and were looked upon as "Johnny come-latelies". We were called "Casuals". I was assigned to the 334th Station Hospital in New Guinea, but I was on tdy (temporary duty) most of my tour. It was at the end of my overseas stint that I found that the 334th was not a figment of my imagination. I joined it in Japan where it had been transferred for occupation duty. Because we were casuals, we had identification problems, never really belonging to anyone. And because we were replacements, we idled away a lot of precious days waiting for assignments.

Novaliches was a large stucco building. A wide entrance opened into a cavernous great-hall surrounded by covered cloisters. One could picture the monks, in their long hooded robes and sandals, living, working, meditating in this place of history that would now house us. The outer perimeter of the cloisters was open with columns and horseshoe arches. At one end of the great hall was a massive fireplace. On either side of the fireplace ascended a broad, stone staircase curving up to the second level. There a wide hall ran the length of the building giving access to small cells on one side of the hall and an open balcony on the other side. The balcony continued around the entire outside perimeter of the building. The outer cell wall was open to the balcony. The monastery was not ornate with tiles, carvings and frescoes, but it reflected the Hispano-Moresque influence in its architecture.

Novaliches Dam, Reservoir, and a town by that name can be found on the maps, but I have been unable to pinpoint where the monastery was located. The reservoir was one of the links in Manila's water supply. The dams and the reservoirs were critical, and there was much fighting trying to disrupt their flow to Manila.

I was assigned to a small bare cell with four other girls. The room was equipped with army cots and mosquito netting. Placed at intervals, on the balcony, were tripods supporting large, black, canvas bags, called Lister[13] bags, that contained our drinking supply. The water was purified with halogen tablets, a chlorine chemical. It was hot and nasty tasting. That was the extent of the preparations for our arrival. There was no electricity, no running water and no toilet facilities.

How many of you had a little girl who had to inspect the plumbing every time you took her visiting? Well, I was one of those little girls, and now, at Novaliches, I found it very traumatizing to have nothing to inspect. Eventually, it became imperative to do something about this oversight. Thereupon, three of us embarked upon a pilgrimage. We came to a courtyard outside the building. There we saw some of the soldiers who had drawn the duty of guarding the nurses. Most of them were younger than we were.

At this time, we hadn't resorted to disappearing into the bush. Like children, we told them of our emergency. One gallant lad assumed the role of Sir Walter Raleigh[14], but rather than spread a cloak for our combat-boot-clad feet, he produced the side of a packing crate. This he impaled in the ground at the outer edge of the compound. The three of us staked out a spot in front of the makeshift partition on the side concealed from the compound. We faced a neglected field that had not completely reverted to jungle. To my eternal dismay, I watched, transfixed, as a huge water buffalo came lumbering across the field straight for our precarious position. Too terrified to move, I remained, still in a squatting stance no less, as he invaded my space, stopping short of upsetting me, packing crate and all. His big nose was no more then a quarter of an inch from mine. His mammoth head was three times bigger than my head. One slurp of his tongue could have washed my whole face. How long we remained there, eyeball to eyeball, I cannot say. I think it was forever. I have no notion of what happened to the two girls beside me. At that moment, nothing existed in the whole, wide world except that water buffalo and me. Probably deciding that I was not a worthy trophy, he lumbered off, no doubt satisfied that he had scared me witless.

A magnificent latrine, one with several holes all in a row, subsequently was built. It had one main drawback. If we didn't troop, en masse, to the latrine and were unfortunate enough to need a solo trip, we had to take an armed escort with us. In the time of my story, young ladies were not accustomed to inviting young men on such an outing. Alas, I was one of the unfortunate ones.

There was usually a roaring fire in the fireplace of the great hall, and it was there that one could find a night guard. Trying to pretend that I was not self-conscious, I would stiffly say, "Soldier, please escort me to the latrine." Whereupon, he would shoulder his weapon, and in stunned silence, we would grope our way down the dark path some distance from the monastery. There he waited to escort me back. God, I hated that!

Of course, I could have used my helmet. We used them for everything else. We washed our clothes in them. We upturned them and sat on them. They were a good carrier for sundries, and, if we became sick to our stomach, well, there was our helmet.

Having gone from ship to jungle to monastery that first exhausting day, our army cots felt like king-size water beds. However, a deep, dreamless sleep was to be denied. Suddenly, the night stillness was punctuated by screams, shots, scrambling feet rushing past on the balcony outside our room. A starving Japanese soldier had crept into the large room at the end of the hall and was rifllng duffle bags when some of the girls awoke. Such was the pandemonium of shrieking, screaming, shouting, and the sound of heavy boots on the balcony, that all sleep was banished. That hapless Japanese had not bargained on a roomful of screaming women. Undoubtedly, he was relieved to be apprehended by our soldiers.

It was August 3, 1945 when our voyage ended, and our interim at the monastery began. In a few short days, word was to come of an event so awesome, and of such historic proportion, as to permanently change our world as we knew it. It was August 6, 1945. We were to hear the electrifying news, signaling the first use of atomic weaponry, of the bombing of Hiroshima on the island of Honshu, Japan. At first shocked, there arose in the throats, of all present that day, a deafening cheer that was likened to a modern day sonic-boom supplanting the vacuum of silence that had greeted the announcement. All, but me. The cheer stuck in my throat. I was humbly grateful that thousands of our boys (and us, too) would be spared from the annihilation that would have resulted from the invasion of the Japanese homeland. Still, I felt no elation. We would live, all of us, with the horror of atomic potential forevermore.

A second bomb was detonated over Nagasaki on the island of Kyushu, Japan, on August 9, 1945.

On the fiftieth anniversary of the atomic destruction of those two cities, there was much debate by the generation, as yet unborn at the time of this story, about the ethics of our country doing such a horrendous thing. Using "ethics" and "war" in the same sentence is an incongruity. The tone of these "hindsighters" took on a sinister character as they castigated the leadership and the country for their "barbarism and cruelty". The revisionist consensus was that the whole conflict was our fault and perpetuated by us. The personal interviews between old veterans and young commentators, that I witnessed, dripped with sarcasm and contempt in an attempt to humiliate the veterans. What needs to be understood is that the Japanese had two million men on the homeland ready to fight to the death; that they had been conditioned by their leaders to never surrender; that every advantage of topography was utilized with beefed up defenses; that the whole of Japan was honeycombed with pillboxes; that they were prepared to crush us with a fanaticism unknown in the American psyche.

Our forces were spread between two fronts, a world apart from each other. We were three thousand miles from Europe and the nine thousand miles from the Pacific Theater, necessitating many thousands in support of the fighting troops, the ratio usually being ten to one. Our willingness to leave home and fight on foreign soil spared an invasion of our homeland, and make no mistake, the Japanese were so certain of victory that they had printed American currency to flood our markets with bogus bills to ruin and enslave our economy.

I am not making a case for atomic weaponry, but the use of it hastened the end of the war. The Japanese War Minister, Anami, wanted to fight to the death. Foreign Minister Togo was more inclined to accept the articles of surrender. On August 15, 1945, Emperor Hirohito went on the air for the first time in history to inform the people of the surrender. The situation was awkward, first, because the word "surrender" was unknown in the warriors' vocabulary, and secondly, the Japanese people, kept in ignorance about the true course of events, thought their emperor was going to order them to fight to the last man. They considered that edict "divine ordinance" and were prepared to carry it out. Stunned by the true nature of the emperor's announcement, there followed nationwide weeping and wailing and mass suicide outside the emperor's palace. War Minister Anami and a group of officers plotting a coup d'etat against the emperor were among the suicides.

It must be remembered that the Japanese people were never told that it was they who attacked us at Pearl Harbor. They were given to understand that we started the war, and they were called upon to defend their homeland from the "evil hordes" who would overrun them. It was not until the interest generated by the fiftieth anniversary observances that the people were finally told of their role in the conflict. Many were in denial, unable to accept the truth of their complicity.

In June of 1995, Japan's ruling coalition balked at a resolution of apology, but compromised on a declaration of "deep remorse" for "acts of aggression" against Asian nations. On August 15, 1995, Premier Tomiichi Murayama in a televised speech, offered a "heartfelt apology" for his country's acts of "colonial rule and aggression" against other countries in World War II. It is not clear whether the United States is included in that apology. This act was the first time that a Japanese leader used the word "apology" in regards to the war

Government factions and Japanese veterans groups are not in accord with Murayama and continue their reluctance to acknowledge their role as an aggressor in the war or their brutal occupation in Japanese held countries, including South Korea, China, and the Philippines. In the Japanese mind, to do so would bring dishonor on the military.

An excerpt from Murayama's speech follows:

Colonial Rule, Aggresslon Cited

"In his speech, Murayama said, "During a certain period in the not too distant past Japan, following a mistaken national policy, advanced along the road to war, only to ensnare the Japanese people in a fateful crisis, and through its colonial rule and aggression caused tremendous damage and suffering to the people of many countries, particularly to those of Asian nations." The premier did not cite any specific acts of aggression.

The premier continued, "In the hope that no such mistake be made in the future, I regard, in a spirit of humility, these irrefutable facts of history, and express here once again my feelings of deep remorse and state my heartfelt apology."

Murayama emphasized that Japan itself was a victim in the war, "as the only country to have experienced the devastation of atomic bombing." He avoided mentioning the U.S. in the context of the bombing, but thanked the U.S. for its "indispensable support and assistance" to Japan in helping the country rebuild itself after the war.

Murayama contended that the only way Japan could "atone for its past and lay to rest the spirits of those who perished" would be to "actively strive to further global disarmament in areas such as the strengthening of the nuclear nonproliferation regime."

From "Facts on File" Vol.55, no. 2856 - August 24, 1995

A government keeping a populace in the dark for fifty years about their heinous attack on us is the ultimate in managed news.

We are not a bellicose nation, but when called upon to save the peoples, and yes, the entire historical cultures of Europe, and to preserve our homeland from invasion, we moved in concert with valor and perseverance. While busy with the exigencies of daily living, I had never given much thought to what was accomplished by all of us. But now that I have the luxury of time to reflect, I am exceedingly proud of us. My generation was something special, and when we're all gone, the world will be a sorrier place.

With nothing more challenging to do, we were usually in our cots at dusk, with our mosquito netting securely tucked around us. With no electricity, we could not read. Come to think of it, we didn't have anything to read. There were Mary Kay, the girl whose father had died while we were at Camp Anza; Mary Jane, whom I had met at Newton D. Baker; a girl whom I knew only as "Babe"; and a pleasant girl whose name eludes me. The following account concerns the fourth girl:

She was terrified of contracting malaria. She was always first under her mosquito netting long before the little beasts became active at dusk. We were continuing our regimen of Atabrine started while still at sea, but this drug did not protect us from malaria. Its function was to ameliorate the symptoms should we contract it.

Here, I must digress and tell you about my flash light. I was the only one in the whole monastery with a flash light. I had disobeyed orders again while still in Camp Anza, California. We had been told to stow our flash lights in our foot lockers, the same foot locker that never caught up with me. Crossing under blackout conditions, it behooved us to carry nothing that could accidentally expose our position or get in the wrong hands to be used to betray us. For some perverse reason, I kept my flash light with me, vowing complete responsibility for keeping it hidden. When our orders were changed to a hospital ship, no one had access to her foot locker in the hold of the ship to retrieve a flash light.

My flash light gained importance one night when the aforementioned malarial-phobic girl asked to borrow it to illuminate that dark path to the latrine. She was loathe to crawl out from under her netting, but this night, there was an imperative to do so. She returned, sobbing, and related the following, "I couldn't help it. I dropped your flash light in the hole." and then, her sobbing increasing in anguish, she wailed, "And it's still burning!" So went the only flash light in the outfit. There must have some kind of poetic justice in this. I thought I was so smart keeping my flash light, and now it was unavailable like all the rest. Ironically, the girl in my story was the only one of us to contract malaria.

Life at the monastery was primitive. We got a generator that supplied electricity for a limited time in the evening. In the courtyard was a well with an old-fashioned pump. We used our helmets for basins. We still took our drinking water from the Lister bags. Our enterprising guards rigged up a washing machine made from half a wooden keg and fitted it with handcranked wringers. Filling our helmets from the well, we poured the water into the tub. Add some G.I. soap, and we were in business. How little it took to please us. We were delighted with our "new appliance".

It was with some annoyance that I pondered a situation within our group. There was a caste system of rank among the officers, and between officers and enlisted personnel. However, among us, we were all the same rank. We wore identical clothes. No one had material goods that were better than the others. We had the same purpose for being here, and we were sharing the same life experience. So why would anybody steal my clothes off the clothesline? I would busy myself washing clothes in our brand new washing machine, and I would hang them up in the yard where lines had mysteriously appeared. Every time I retrieved my laundry, several items would be missing. It was more disappointing to me that there were those in short supply of honesty than there was concern for any lost items.

By some psychic telepathy, it wasn't long before word spread that there was a monastery full of nurses up in the hills. Soon, swarms of swains poured into Novaliches. This necessitated instituting rules of signing in and out, of a curfew, and a listing of the name and outfit of any officer taking us out. Inasmuch as we couldn't leave the monastery without an armed escort, we welcomed this influx of men for giving us the opportunity to get off the grounds. Does today's army look after its female personnel? We felt appreciated and protected, and I liked it. This did not diminish our courage, our strength or our ability to do our job.

The officers who made the trek to this hidden place made our days more exciting. I could not quote any ratio, but we women were vastly outnumbered. Any women whose nature it was to form liasons with the opposite sex, had ample opportunity. I cannot recall how dates were made. We did not have a telephone. Did they come, look the crop over and pick one like shopping in a modern day super-market? That concept was repugnant to me.

One evening, I had a date with a major. Did some advance guy come up to me and say, "Look. I got this major who hasn't seen a white woman for months. I gotta fix him up with somebody. He's driving ninety miles south from his outpost to get here." I do not know how the arrangement was made, but the above scenario is as plausible as any, and the above facts pertaining to the major are correct. I had become pretty good at sizing up people, but I bombed on this one.

We went to an officers' club somewhere near Manila. He was gallant and charming until he had imbibed too much, and then he turned surly and mean. He had an enlisted man driver so it did not matter that he was in no condition to drive. He would order his driver to drive on roads chosen at random in very unfamiliar terrain. The roads could accomodate the width of two vehicles, and the jungle rose immediately, impinging close on both sides of the roads.

He wouldn't bring me "home". In America, my father would have met him at the door with his "persona non grata" speech. But Father wasn't here, and I would have to get out of this one by myself. I would order the enlisted man to take me back to the monastery, but the major outranked me, and no way was that boy going to obey me. It got pretty ugly, but I finally made it back to the monastery way past curfew. And after curfew, the guards bristled at the slightest sound. We got the "Halt! or I'll shoot!" treatment. The next day, I had to account for myself with the chief nurse. I was "sentenced" to police the area and pick up all the cigarette butts. Although he was my requisite armed escort, he was not a gentleman, and he jeopardized all of us careening around unknown territory in the jungle. That is one time I wasn't "appreciated or protected." Afterwards, he apologized for his boorish behavior.

One day, a jeep drove into the courtyard and discharged Clenie and Janie back from exile in Leyte. I looked down from the balcony and shrieked, "CLENIE!" "JANIE!" Clenie and I played hopscotch the whole overseas tour, reuniting and separating, but Janie stayed with me until Japan.

And what about Schmitty? She became ill and was hospitalized at Santo Tomas, the ancient Philippine University, that had so recently been the infamous prison to our soldiers and nurses. It was early in 1945, on February 3rd to the 6th, that our American forces liberated Bilibid prison and Santo Tomas during the action to recapture Manila.

Schmitty had asked me to intercept a date she was expecting, and when I did, he offered to take me to see her. I found her in a big, ugly, bare room with no patients occupying the other beds. She looked so forsaken and forlorn. But Schmitty was tough. She gave me one of her jaunty smiles, and we said our goodbyes. I was not to see her again until long after the war.

> Santo Tomas University was founded in 1605 by Dominican missionaries in the ancient medieval city of Intramuros, the original Manila. A portion of it still occupies the first building that dates from 1611.

Mary Jane and I received permission to hitch a ride on the mail truck on its return trip to Manila. The city showed the wear and tear of war, poverty, disease and a collapse of its infrastructure. Three-sided stalls faced dusty, debris-littered sidewalks. There always seemed to be commotion in the streets with throngs of displaced people begging or hawking tawdry goods. Mary Jane and I felt like Pied Pipers[15] as gangs of street urchins followed us everywhere, their numbers growing like flies attracted to a carcass. Glancing backward at them, they resembled a huge swarm all glued together and moving as one. We hurried along as their begging got bolder until, finally, the leaders got a hold on the waistbands of our slacks and began ripping them off our persons, yelling, "You sella these? You sella these?" The last thing I saw as we sprinted to outrun them was Mary Jane, hanging on to her slacks half stripped from her body, hitching them up as she ran. We were winded and shaken after our escape from the mob. Although these street urchins were victims of war, they were far from harmless little children.

Parched from the heat, dust and our exertion, we realized we had not brought our canteens. One rule, set in stone, was not to drink anything except the purified water at the military facilities. A sad story that had come to our attention shortly after our arrival was that of some army doctors and nurses who had received their orders for stateside duty. They went night-clubbing to celebrate their going home, had drunk the local offering of "gook-juice", and died. Any club that was not an army sanctioned officers' or enlisted mens' club was suspect. One of the street stalls displayed a bottled drink labeled "sarsparilla", but we were afraid to chance it.

It was then that we hatched the scheme to go down to the harbor and hitch a ride on a launch out to one of the navy ships at anchor in the bay. A navy ship would be the only place where we could get purified water. We had no trouble finding a launch that would transport us. It didn't matter what ship we were going to. Any one of them would do. We climbed the ship's ladder, and after asking permission, we were piped aboard according to navy protocol. We were soon surrounded by navy men. I guess I hadn't realized that we were a novelty, especially in a zone where American women were not a common sight.

We not only got a drink of water, we were taken to dinner in their mess. We had heard that the navy ate well, but this was like a kid pressing her nose against the candy store window and getting invited inside. There were white cloths on the table; our utensils were real flatware; we ate from real dishes, not metal mess kits. They hovered around us, waited on us, but the piece de resistance was real ice cream. I sat there wishing that I were dressed for dinner, or at the very least, I wished that I were clean and had some lipstick on.

Like two Cinderellas, our idyll was over all too soon. We had to be back to the monastery at the stroke of ten. It was dark by now and launch traffic was curtailed until daybreak. I panicked at the thoughts of patrols going out to look for us if we were presumed missing. To solve the dilemma, the admiral's personal launch was sent over from his ship, and we rode to shore in style. With the men vying for attention, we had no trouble getting escorts to the monastery. They, of course, had to requisition a jeep, drive an hour to our isolated home in the hills, and back again. I do not presume that the admiral's launch was waiting for them.

Mary Jane and I saw them several times. We spent one lazy, dreamlike evening in a funny, little cafe built on stilts, open on all four sides and covered with a roof of thatch. It was nothing more than bamboo furniture with candles on the tables, the kind where the wax has run all over the bottles so the light looks as if it were emanating from a prehistoric blob. A Filipino mamma moved around unobtrusively. We just sat there in a sort of inertia with no air disturbing the smoke plume from the candle as it lazily floated up into the sultry night. Such was the mood as I sat there vacantly staring off into space until my eyes focused on Mary Jane. Something in her demeanor alerted me. She was gazing at her fella with a look of complete devotion. I whispered to Joe, my escort, "Mary Jane has fallen hard. I don't want her to get hurt. Is he married?", and Joe confessed that Mary Jane's love interest was, indeed, married. As an afterthought, I turned to Joe and asked him if he, too, was married. He said, "Yes." Well, that was that. They were both personable men, but it was not my practice to knowingly date a married man. I know how I would feel if I were a wife waiting for my man to come home, and he was living it up with a service woman. Also, it is patently unfair to the girl far from home to be deluded into thinking that the man is sincere, as was the case with Mary Jane.

There was always commotion in the streets with throngs of displaced people, begging or hawking tawdry goods.

The Palace

On one occasion, an escape from the confines of the monastery with my armed escort led to an adventure I enjoy remembering. My companion, a young lieutenant, and I headed for nowhere in particular. Understand that there were not many places to go, or places that it would be safe to go. War torn Manila had little to offer. One had to know the location of hastily erected officers' clubs. The Filipino bars with their offering of "gook juice", the native equivalent of moonshine, were off limits. But it was a nice day without rain (the rainy season would soon be upon us.) so we settled for an afternoon drive, such a drive being no luxury in a jeep over rough roads. At some point, he stopped the jeep and asked for some tips on how to kill some more time. We had stopped near an important looking, big white building which was surrounded by a high white wall. I recognized it as the president's palace. "Wouldn't it be fun to see the palace?" "I dare you." "Go with me." "Let's do it!" so I goaded him. Our plan was brazen but simple: we would stand straight and tall and try to look like some important personages on official business.

We sallied forth, gave a snappy salute to the guard at the main gate and swept by leaving a bewildered soldier in our wake. So far, so good. We were now on the grounds of a large estate. There was a walk, maybe twelve feet wide, that ran around the entire inner perimeter. Spaced at intervals along its length were small vertical guard shelters such as the little pointy-roofed structures housing a wooden soldier that one has seen in a child's book. But these guard houses were not toys, and the armed Philippine soldiers standing beside each one were not made of wood.

A quick glance told us that we must traverse several hundred feet past many guards, any one of which might challenge us before we reached the palace. Our boots didn't exactly sound like stormtroopers'[16], but they did make an impressive staccato as we marched in cadence up the walk, saluting each guard as we passed. Could we maintain our imperious demeanor for just a little bit longer? It seemed like an eternity, but there it was, the palace. We had reached our objective, but were we trading one peril for another? We hurled ourselves through the big main door into a huge, cool, white marble foyer. All at once, our resolve crumpled. I could feel my shoulders sag and the air drain from my chest. It would be a relief to get caught - almost. Even if we weren't discovered, how could we leave the way we had come and run that gauntlet again? Before our eyes could readjust from the bright sunlight; before we could shift our brains back in gear, we heard hurried footsteps rushing down the wide marble staircase that fed into the foyer. With sinking hearts, we knew the charade was over.

Presently, a young Chinese man appeared. He was impeccably dressed in elegant business attire. With his brow furrowed in alarm, he sputtered, "Who? You? What?" It seemed to have occurred to him that he had placed himself in jeopardy confronting an unknown presence without military backup. We sensed it prudent to throw ourselves on his mercy. I hoped he had a sense of the ludicrous. We confessed the entire plot. His eyes widened in disbelief. Then comprehending the daring of our trespass, his face ringed in smiles, and he erupted into laughter as if he were a co-conspirator. "Come on." he said, "I'll show you around."

He told us that he was the president's private secretary. He took us on an extensive palace tour. I was impressed most by the grand ballroom and the state dining room. The secretary pointed out the magnificent crystal chandeliers from Czechoslovakia that were spaced at intervals along the full length of the ceilings. He showed where the bullets had crashed through them during the assault on Manila.

The opulence of the palace was in startling contrast to the poverty of the country. It seemed incongruous to me that, in the midst of deprivation and suffering, there were those who were insulated from the relentless struggle for survival. I was still learning that this was so throughout the societies of man.

Our guide terminated the tour by ushering us into his private quarters. He served a delightful lunch, tempting our palates with gourmet goodies (in particular, I remember little, succulent sandwiches of crab-meat and soft, decadent white bread) that were certain to ruin us for army fare. We left the palace as V.I.P.'s as if we had every right to be there. It was in stark contrast to our unauthorized "breaking and entering."

I sometimes think of that young lieutenant. I don't even know his name. I never saw him again. He was probably still shaken by his brush with lawlessness, and was fearful of any further contact with that girl who was apt to brew up another daredevil escapade. I wonder, did he grow old with the rest of us? Did he ever recall the time that he and his partner in derring-do stormed the president's palace?

This is a brief orientation of some political highlights surrounding the Philippine government and the occupants of the palace:

In the spring of 1941, Manuel Quezon was president of the Philippines. He and Sergio Osmena were re-elected to the presidency and vice-presidency in November 1941.

In December, they fled Manila for Corregidor and there were inaugurated for a second term.

By February 1942, Washington announced that the Philippine government was "functioning somewhere in the Philippines."

On May 7, 1942, Japan had announced complete control of the Philippines and had set up a puppet government.

On May 14, 1942, President Quezon and Vice-President Osmena established a government in exile in Washington D.C.

President Quezon died at Saranac Lake, New York on August 1, 1944. Vice-President Osmena became president of the Philippine Commonwealth in exile.

On October 21, 1944, President Osmena, together with his cabinet, accompanied the American invasion forces to Leyte.

General MacArthur announced the capture of Leyte's capital, Tacloban, on October 22, 1944, which became the temporary capital of the Philippine Commonwealth.

By February 16, 1945, American troops recaptured Corregidor, and by February 24, 1945, the last of the Japanese garrison in Manila was destroyed.

Three days later, on February 27, 1945, the control of the civil government of the Philippines, having returned to its rightful capital, Manila, was turned over to President Osmena by General MacArthur.

At the time of our unauthorized "visit" to the palace, in August of 1945, General MacArthur announced that complete civil administration would begin on September 1, 1945. Fortunately for us, the president was "not at home" the day of our trepass. The only thing that I have learned outside of my very personal and private tour of the "Malacanang Palace" is that it has fifty-four rooms.

The Surrender

The indolence of life at the monastery was palling on me. It was not for this that I had joined the army. The most nursing and the best nursing I had done thus far was at Newton D. Baker. I am proud of what I had done there. But here, the idleness was corrupting. Idleness makes for mischief, and I confess that I was not immune to mischief.

The rumor mill was busy spieling out nebulous facts that we took for gospel. One of the rumors concerned a Japanese surrender, but wasn't the concept of surrender foreign to the Japanese mind? Still, the Japanese war machine was almost depleted. They could no longer reach far-flung troops with supplies; living off the devastated land was meager at best; and the atom bomb had destroyed two of their cities.

The Japanese general in this story was acutely aware of the collapse of the Japanese forces. He wrestled with the difficult decision of shaming his starving men by surrendering them to the Americans, or of stubbornly fighting to the death.

I chose to give credence to the surrender whispers. I had been conditioned by my father to avail myself of every educational opportunity. This was educational. Right? This was historical. Right? All this, I told to my commanding officer. She must have been impressed by my earnestness, "my scholarship". Her only condition was that I have an armed escort. I lied, shamelessly, so desperately did I want to go, and I assured her that, in fact, I had taken care of that provision in anticipation of her permission. I had a partner in deception, a cellmate, Babe. Her name, "Babe", had always conjured a picture of a gum-chewing, wise-cracking, overly made-up, blowzy, bottle blonde. Not so with this Babe. She was a sweet, soft-spoken, genteel lady. Why she ever agreed to accompany me in my idiocy, I could never fathom, and so together, we began our ill-advised adventure.

Rumor had it that the surrender ceremony was "somewhere north" of our present position. Babe and I left the security of our compound and found a road that seemed to be going in the right general direction. No matter that I had no sense of direction. I had passed map-reading, hadn't I? The road was narrow with the dense jungle reaching out to engulf it. We slogged along in a driving rain. So copious were the deluges during the rainy season that we were inadequately protected by our trench coats. With the fearlessness and the arrogance of youth, I believed, with every fiber of my body, that I could fend off an enemy assault with my Philippine dagger......as long as there were not too many of them. I thought my dagger was an exquisite tool. It had a carved, ebony handle inlaid with steel. There must be a name for the eight inch, two-sided blade. It was an undulating, "squiggling" blade, and looked wicked enough. Ah, this was the time of our lives when we were immortal and invincible.

We had mushed along, silently, for some distance. The driving force of the rain made conversation difficult. If either of us harbored misgivings, we didn't betray them to each other. The narrow ribbon of road was awash from the downpour. There was no traffic, not even an ox cart, that ventured forth. We passed no village, or isolated hut, to remind us of civilization, only dense jungle that concealed anything lurking within. Our isolation was complete. The silence was broken only by the rain when, suddenly, I was alerted to a new sound. My ears twitched, and my jaws contracted the way they do when you suck a lemon. The sound? A vehicle motor off in the distance? My heart and stomach fused into one and rose in my throat. Should we hide in the jungle? Stay on the road? The vehicle just might be one of ours. I think that both of us had concluded, privately, that we were in need of rescuing.

A jeep loomed into view. Ours! The wet road steamed with scalded rubber as the jeep screeched to a halt at the sight of two half-drowned waifs - female waifs. A colonel, about the vintage of my father, and his driver stared at us in disbelief. Then the rain storm was rent by a fury and a barrage of profanity such as I had never heard before. "What in the (expletive-expletive) do you think you are doing alone in the jungle?" We told him, with a wide-eyed innocence mastered only by our species, that we were going to the surrender. Sketchy as our information had been, there was, indeed, a surrender that day, and the northerly direction had been correct.

The colonel was heading for the same destination. He had reached the point of no return. He couldn't take us back where we belonged (and certain disciplinary action), or he would miss the appointed time. With utter disgust, he resigned himself to taking us with him. I made the rest of the trip in a taut silence, contemplating my fingernails, not daring to look at him. In all the years since, I have never seen a man as angry as that frustrated colonel.

But, was it not providential that we were rescued from our folly?

We arrived at a remote infantry outpost commanded by a weather-beaten, redhaired, blue-eyed colonel. Unlike the colonel who was our reluctant "babysitter", the big redhead was delighted to see us. His affable demeanor belied what he and his men had been through. Within the limitations of his primitive post, he was gracious and solicitous. He fed us. He rounded up donations of dry clothing from his men. He insisted that I trade my soaked boots for a pair of his shoes. I could have put both my feet in one of his shoes. But, he made us feel special.

I liked him immediately. I have thought many times since then how touching was his eagerness to care for us. I realized how hungry he and his men were for some femininity, and I felt that he was doing for us what he would hope someone would do for his family in similar straits. I never perceived that he had any designs on me other than paternalistic, and I fell right into it, enjoying a surrogate father.

He told Babe and me that, yes indeed, we could go to the surrender. One prohibition was that we were not to get out of the jeep or call attention to ourselves in any way. I could see the sternness of command behind that kind face. He had no cause for concern. I could scarcely move in his big shoes and the big clumsy clothes borrowed from his soldiers.

The appointed time had arrived. We caravanned to a clearing in the jungle. As if on cue, the rain stopped. The colonel's troops were in formation at one end of the clearing. A general had arrived from headquarters in Manila. The air was thick and suffocating. The jungle was motionless. Suddenly, swiftly, the Japanese general appeared in the clearing as if he were an apparition moving through the jungle without a sound. His troops moved into the clearing just as quietly as if they had slid through the dense growth. They lined up at attention behind their general. Staring straight ahead, these men remained the inscrutable Japanese. Most were in tatters. All were wearing the regulation Japanese uniform headgear. They stood rigidly at attention. I can only guess their fear and shame. They were a credit to their general.

Our troops had snapped to attention at the appearance of the Japanese general. He surrendered his sword to the ranking officer. The American general was not unfeeling and accorded every courtesy commensurate with the Japanese general's rank. He offered the sword back to the surrendering officer and seemed to be attempting some conciliatory remarks. The Japanese general rejected the offer of the return of his sword. Without dropping the mantle of his rank, he stepped smartly into a waiting vehicle that was not unlike our police paddy wagon. I think our men recognized a worthy adversary, a gallant general, and in some inverted way, wanted to convey the thought that they understood. I was proud of the way our men had handled, with dignity and respect, the men who had recently been their brutal enemies. Perhaps, respect is the first step in overcoming hatred.

Babe and I need not have been admonished to keep a low profile. We were subdued and very moved by what we had witnessed. I do not think that an Occidental can fully appreciate the courage of the Japanese general in resisting the temptation to accept the return of his sword. Both of us knew that we had witnessed a piece of history.

I was to meet the blue-eyed colonel again.

> I entertained the idea that I could put names on the players in this drama. To that end, I visited the National Military Archives in College Park, Maryland. The after action reports during the period in question, early August, 1945, were revealing and fascinating, but they did not yield what I sought.
>
> The study of maps named the Sixth Army, commanded by General Krueger, as the main force in

the area. He and his army had fought up the coast of New Guinea to its western tip establishing land bases for American airmen. The humid green coast was solid with supply and naval bases.

It was time for General Krueger to go northward. He captured Morotai in the Halmaheras and established the final island air base within striking distance of the Philippines.

Now he was ready to mount one of the greatest campaigns in the war, the liberation of the Philippines. Leyte, almost in the center of the archipelago, was the first target. An armada of more than six hundred ships along with the Sixth Army hit Leyte on October 20, 1944. There followed the biggest and toughest battle fought by the men of the Sixth Army up to that time. The battle raged for two months "across coastal rice paddies, through valley swamps and in mountain mud" (quoted from archival reports.).

The army moved inexorably north, taking Mindoro and nearby Marinduque, toward Luzon and the avenging of Bataan and Corregidor. General MacArthur had set January 9, 1945 as D-Day to launch the Luzon campaign. The battle was long and hard, fought through the central plains, through mountains in the north and east, and in the southern provinces. The Sixth Army entered Manila on February 3, 1945. Corregidor was recaptured by a daring air and sea assault on February 16, 1945.

It was not until June 1945, six months into the battle for Luzon, after hard fighting with an enemy firmly entrenched in the mountains, that the American forces broke through the mountain passes into the Cagayan Valley and brought a hard won victory to the Battle of Luzon.

There followed mopping up operations. It was within the first half of August that my friend and I had set out on our foolhardy adventure, and it was in that time frame, August 15, 1945 that the Japanese surrender order had gone out to its troops.

The archival reports covering August 1945 into September 1945 - and they are by no means complete - give an overview of the continuing action. Vigorous patrols encountered stubborn pockets of resistance. It was interesting to note that, in addition to enemy casualties and captures, tallies of prisoners surrendered by their commanders were included in all reports. Never were the commanding officers identified. Surrenders were occurring both before and after the August 15 order, but the greatest number laid down their arms on the day designated for a cease fire. Prisoners were surrendering faster than collection points could be set up.

I had hoped that I could name both men, the general on General Krueger's staff, who had come from Manila and the Japanese general. The surrender of the highest ranking Japanese general, General Yamashita, is well documented. A formal ceremony was held at the Philippine summer capital of Baguio, on September 3, 1945. As for the lesser generals involved in the ceremony I witnessed, I shall probably never know their identities.

It is noteworthy that, after the liberation of the Philippines, General Krueger was to lead the Sixth Army in the attack on the Japanese mainland. The greatest amphibious attack in history was to have been made in November 1945 with 800,000 men who would face a foe of 2,000,000 Japanese firmly entrenched in their homeland.

I will not even speculate what the outcome might have been had that military operation been necessary.

The Blue-eyed Colonel

I was poor in orientating to time spans. It seemed as if we had been detained at the monastery longer than approximately two weeks. Orders came swiftly without prior warning. The temporary nature of our existence was hard on me. Systematically, I would rush around tying up tag ends. I secured all of Schmitty's belongings and fussed that I wouldn't be there to see that she got her gear. I left messages with the O.D. (Officer of the Day) to pass along to any of my male friends who came to call. It distressed me that some of the girls were absent from the monastery, and I didn't get a chance to say my good-byes. This proclivity of mine to tend to details was a good indication of why I was always late. We were going to Manila, and Janie would be going with me. Clenie's assignment took her away again.

We were billeted in a former boys' school. Our cots were set up in one of the classrooms. I suppose it was nicer and better appointed than Novaliches, but I rather missed that ancient structure. There was a romanticism and an aura about the monastery. I could imagine our soprano laughter joining the echoes of other eras when it sheltered other lives and existed for other purposes.

I was going on duty! I recall a long approach leading to an impressive, yellow stucco building. Jeeps picked us up every morning and transported us there. My orders said only "tdy Base K" but I think the large hospital was Manila General Hospital, and now it was housing American military personnel. I cannot claim to have done any gratifying nursing there. I never knew to which ward I would be assigned until I reported for duty every morning. As a result, there was no follow up with any of my patients. About the only thing I got out of duty there was being exposed to a new kind of penicillin that used beeswax for its vehicle. That had been developed in the few short months since my Odyssey[17] had begun. Apparently, it never became standard practice, and I never saw it again. I saw a familiar face in the person of a dentist whom I had met at Camp Beale. I had made an appointment with him for a dental check, but I was whisked away again before I could keep it.

During my brief interim at Manila General, I was surprised to learn someone was waiting for me at the boys' school. It was the blue-eyed colonel. By what wizardry the men could track us down, I never knew. They had access to information that eluded us. He had plans for Babe and me. He always brought an escort for Babe, and I doubt that he had any difficulty getting a volunteer for the assignment. Among our outings, one is indelibly imprinted in my memory.

Very early, he had come to take us to a Filipino birthday party. The family was more affluent than most. Their house was larger, with two stories, the upper floor consisting of two rooms, a living room and a dining room. Most Filipino houses were built on stilts, had one room, with the entrance being gained by a bamboo ladder that could be pulled into the room at night. The house to which we were invited was raised off the ground slightly by stilts to keep out crawly things and water during the rainy season. The outside walls were open except for a waist high solid railing. The floors were bare and the only furniture were straight-back chairs which lined two sides of the room. The men sat on one side and the women on the other.

Babe and I sat there with pleasant expressions pasted on our faces trying to look responsive. We didn't understand the language, but we pretended we were participating. Meanwhile, the colonel moved easily among the guests, chatting in their language, greeting and acknowledging everyone. It was obvious that they held him in high esteem and were flattered by his presence.

That part of the ritual over, everyone retired to the dining room. There a large table was so heavily laden with food that one suspected they had a secret source. The colonel always prompted us on protocol, and in this instance, he whispered that we must eat everything they served us. Aside from the volume of food being beyond my capacity, I was concerned about sanitation. I didn't want to get what was indelicately referred to as the "G.I. Trots".

The festivities were over, but the colonel had another stop to make. He had recently brought his men south to

Manila, but a skeleton force was maintaining the outpost. It was this outpost he would check on. He had told Babe and me to bring our bathing suits. Now, why would anyone bring a bathing suit to a war? However, like the Scout motto "Be Prepared.", I had thrown one in my luggage, and apparently so had Babe.

In the vicinity of the outpost were the remains of what must have been a spa. The swimming pool was still intact, so Babe and I donned our suits for a swim while the colonel tended to his men. We continued to be a curiosity. While Babe and I were cavorting in the water, we became aware of a growing gathering at pool side. Soon, all four sides of the pool were solid with native spectators. They stared at us with such unabashed frankness that we became acutely embarrassed. Neither one of us wanted to exit the pool and push our way through them. We felt so exposed that we might as well have been naked. We resorted to staying submerged save for our heads until the colonel came and called out, "Come on, girls. The boys have prepared a special feast for you." We should have welcomed a departure from dehydrated, reconstituted food, but both of us groaned inwardly. The birthday meal was weighing heavily on us, but there it was, another chicken dinner.

The men were so proud of their efforts and waited expectantly for our approval. We murmured the appropriate "Ohs" and "Ahs" and tried our best to do justice to the meal. They reminded me of a bunch of kids cooking breakfast on Mother's Day, so eager were they to please.

Many times it seemed to me that we were wearing other hats in addition to that of the Army Nurse Corps. One of them was that of Morale Officer. I didn't mind the role. Just our being there brought the soldiers a touch of home.

Gluttony was not one of my sins, but there I was, with Babe, bloated and uncomfortable. Even so, the colonel had something else in store for us. Erelong, we were back in the jeep bouncing along over the rough roads - hardly a prescription for settling a sick stomach.

It had grown quite late when the colonel brought us to a little hut in the jungle. We were expected. The small interior was lit by a single lantern, and beyond the reaches of its feeble glow, everything receded into the shadows like a Rembrandt[18] painting. A little Filipino woman was puttering around in what served as the kitchen. With a devilish grin, the colonel told us that we were honored guests for dinner, a chicken dinner. Babe and I were close to becoming severely ill, but the colonel cut us no slack. He whispered that we had to eat whatever was offered to us. To refuse would be a serious breach of etiquette. Don't ask. Babe I were on the ragged edge of humiliating the colonel in front of our host by losing our dinner. To this day, my gag reflex responds when I recall three chicken dinners, BIG chicken dinners, each following on the heels of the one before.

Before our disasterous meal, our host had emerged from behind a flap of cloth that covered an interior opening. He was a tall, handsome man with a full head of wavy, steel grey hair and heavy, dark brows. He in no way resembled the natives, but rather showed the Spanish influence in his characteristics. He had a regal bearing that seemed out of place in the homely little hut.

The two men exchanged a few words. They were quiet and subdued. From their whispered conversation, I could not tell in what language they were speaking. They were both tall good-looking men, but the difference in their coloring was startling. The dark one was a captain in the Filipino guerrilla army. He had neither spoken to us or looked in our direction.

Presently, he left the room. As silently as he had left, he reappeared. I could picture him slipping through the jungle eluding the enemy.

Without a word, there in the dim light of the lantern, he stood before me. His arms stretched out to me. Across his upturned palms lay a sword, a Samurai sword. He inclined his body toward me in a slight bow. With great ceremony, he presented the sword to me. I was mesmerized. I do not know what I did. Protest? Thank him? Commit a faux pas by offering it back to him? I was so overcome by this gesture that I have no idea how I comported myself.

The sword has been one of my treasures ever since that eventful day, as much for the circumstances surrounding how it came into my possession as for any intrinsic value it may have.

The Samurai were the feudal warriors of Japan prior to the revolution of 1867-1868 at which time feudalism was abolished. The Samurai sword was symbolic of the Samurai class. The swords of antiquity were made by master sword makers, and they were handed down through the generations and were treasured as part of the family heritage. Some were very ornate with jeweled hilts and were protected in ornate scabbards. The "working swords" had a plain hilt while the lavishly jeweled ones were used for ceremonial purposes. Sometimes, the jeweled hilt would be removed and replaced with a plain hilt if it was going to be used in battle. The antique blades were made of very thin layers of steel fused together by hammering each successive layer. During World War II, factory manufactured swords were issued to the officers.

We have determined that the sword presented to me is antique. In certain light, one can distinguish the very slight irregularities in the blade such as would be present in a hand hammered blade. Also, upon removing the hilt, Japanese characters are visible on the tine. In my attempts to get the characters translated, I have learned the identity of some which seem to reference to the family and the sword maker. However, complete translation has not been possible because the characters are too old to be recognized in the language of modern Japanese.

I have dreamt about learning the identity of the family in Japan and of returning the sword to them.

Everything Babe and I did seemed to give the colonel pleasure. Our chattering, our laughter, our incredulity at things new and revealed to us......our youth...... he found refreshing. His hearty laughter at some of our foibles lifted him out of himself. Babe's escort was always in tow, and his presence made our outings more enjoyable for both of them. After dark, I would drive the Jeep while the colonel dozed. He was too trusting, given my faulty sense of direction. He would insist that I tuck my hair up into a fatigue cap thereby presenting an enlisted man's silhouette as I drove. I do not recall having curfews such as were enforced at the monastery.

One day, the colonel came alone, and Babe was not included. He had another surprise, or so he said. I was suspicious because he was not above playing practical jokes. He took me to the firing range where his men were shooting requalifying rounds. He said he was going to teach me how to shoot. It was a convenient oversight on my part not to reveal that I was a crack shot with medals to back me up. I let him explain the whole procedure, nodding in assent when he asked me if I was game to try.

The rifle we would be using was the M-1, the standard piece of the infantry man. The Enfield and the O-7 were the choice of the sniper, and the light-weight Carbine was a convenient piece for the M.P.s (Military Police). Also, the Carbine was carried by noncombatants for protection when their duties took them to the front.

The range for this shoot was three-hundred yards. In front of the targets was an eight to ten foot deep trench that ran past all the targets on the range. There the spotters stayed protected from the live ammunition hitting the targets overhead. The spotters had long wands with a black disk on one end. After a round had been fired, they would hold up the wand, placing the disk over the bullet hole. The value of the shot was determined by which black, concentric circle the bullet had pierced, the highest value being the bull's-eye in dead center.

I took my place on the firing line. The M-1 was a little heavy for me, but I had learned not to fatigue my muscles by trying to hold it steady. It swayed and I swayed with it, squeezing the trigger the instant the sight was on the bull's-eye. I fired rapid fire and all the positions, and the black disk from the spotter was always where I wanted it. It was then that I learned about the conspiracy. Everybody was in on it, the colonel, the spotters and the men. They were going to have a little fun at my expense.

Here was the plan: the colonel telephoned the spotter on his field phone with instructions to put the disk on the bull's-eye no matter where the bullet went. It wasn't long before the spotter called the colonel and said, "Hell, Colonel, I don't have to *pretend* she's hitting the bull's-eye. She is." The colonel had egg on his face, and the men, those near enough to me to see how the joke had backfired, started leaving the firing range muttering things like, "I don't have to stay here and have some girl outshoot me."

The colonel, surprised and pleased, decided that I should duplicate my prowess on the light-weight Carbine. The range for this shoot was two-hundred yards, and the outcome was the same. Of the three ratings, marksman, sharpshooter, and expert, I had qualified for expert, albeit an unofficial record, inasmuch as I was a noncombatant. I had to "fess up" to the fact that my marksmanship was no accident.

The colonel doted on me as if I were some sprite that he could indulge and thoroughly spoil. The frame of reference in which I still placed myself was that of the "Great Katrinka" although I admit it was a new experience to have approval for everything I did. My own father, who had a greater emotional stake in me, and was fearful of encouraging my recalcitrance, never relaxed his stern visage. He kept his pride in me well hidden lest any overt approval should make me bolder. Knowing that I would receive them, he rerouted all compliments through Mother. I'll wager that the colonel was stern with his own family, but with me, he could afford the luxury of pampering.

His active brain was dreaming up more events. I was to be mascot of his troops. To that end, he had planned a big party to which everyone would be invited, officers and enlisted men alike. And then it happened. The most predictable thing about the army was unpredictability. I got my orders to move on.

I had come off duty at the big, yellow hospital when I received word to hurry back to our quarters and pack up. We were pulling out immediately, that afternoon. I was sick. How could I leave without a word? Just to disappear as if the whole interlude with the colonel had been a fantasy?

Out in the bright sunlight, waiting for our transportation back to our quarters, I spied a jeep with the insignia of the colonel's outfit on it. I yelled, trying to hail it down and dashed down the road after it. When it halted, I explained my situation to the two G.I.s in the jeep, and asked them to please relay my message to the colonel.

Disconsolate, I sat at the Manila airport, waiting for military transportation......and the colonel came. He had received my message. He looked grave as he held me by the shoulders, his piercing blue eyes committing every nuance of my face to his memory. For the first time, I saw a weariness about him. The spark was gone, and he looked old. I stifled a sob. The tables had turned, and I wanted to comfort him. I had not anticipated the awful wrench of parting. This was the army, - easy come, easy go - but, belatedly, I realized that I cared for him deeply. He was such a decent man, and like me, he embraced life fully, knowing there would be pain along the journey.

The unnatural environs of war and separation from loved ones at home bring people together for comfort and companionship. Was that all? Perhaps, but the feelings that I had acknowledged were pure and abiding. I had known the colonel a scant month, a mere wink in the eons of time, but long enough to have amassed memories that have endured these many years. I would experience poignancy and regret for not having reached out to him instead of permitting him to do so much for me. I took precious little solace out of the fact that having a vital, capricious, young thing around renewed him and distracted him from the weight of command. I never saw him again, but the image of his face is as clear as the first time I met him at a primitive outpost in the hills of Luzon.

The plane lifted off the runway, and my heart ached with the stabbing pains of bereavement.

Fourteen of us flew to Leyte.

Leyte

It was September 15, 1945. How was it that I had lived a lifetime in the few short weeks since we had disembarked at Luzon on August 3, 1945? Hostilities were over. There may have been some isolated hold-outs who could not or would not accept the news of surrender. In the aftermath of the atomic bombings of Hiroshima and Nagasaki, the Japanese command had ordered its far flung troops to cease fire. Fear that the Japanese suicide troops would not comply with the surrender order did not materialize. The logistics of a massive troop transfer from the European Theater to the Pacific Theater was not as urgent, and all of us, who were poised for the ultimate invasion of Japan, could relax and give thanks. The instrument of surrender was signed on the battleship, Missouri, in Tokyo Bay, on September 2, 1945. Occupation troops were already moving into the Japanese mainland. Five days after the formal surrender, the American flag was flying over the American Embassy in Tokyo. It was the same flag that had flown over Washington D.C. on Pearl Harbor Day, December 7, 1941. It had been raised over Rome and Berlin, and it was the flag flying over the surrender signing on the battleship, Missouri.

What would our duties entail now? The vast numbers of us, who had been trained, transported and in place for an invasion, would have to be absorbed into a system that would not be facing incoming truckloads of wounded.

We landed at Tacloban airport and were soon trucked to our duty station in the jungle, the 117th Station Hospital. When one speaks of airports and towns in a place like Leyte, one is speaking of a couple runways, or a few huts lining both sides of a dusty road. If there were places more enterprising, I did not see them. Leyte was primitive and did not have too much to recommend it.

My first acquaintance with the 117th was the nurses' compound. There was a row of good-sized tents that had been installed with semi-permanent wood floors. The canvas sides were rolled up to the roof edge. A dirt road ran in front of the tents. At the end of the compound was a latrine and shower.

The compound was surrounded by a high cyclone fence which was completely covered by green canvas to insure privacy. At the corners of the fence were guard towers. The design was not to keep us in, as in a prison, but to keep any, who would do us harm, out. Guards were always manning the towers, allowing for observation of the whole area. We always knew there was a guard somewhere in the vicinity of the main gate of the compound.

Despite the temporary nature of our life style, we were not guests at a resort. We settled in as quickly as possible. Adapting and readapting to each new situation would get high points on today's "stress-o-meter", but whether for emergencies or normal change, we were conditioned for action.

The first night at the 117th was spent in a communal tent at one end of the nurses' compound. The nurses whom we were replacing would be vacating the station the following day. There wasn't much acknowledgement of each other. We came in and they went out. It was obvious that they were in a hurry to leave.

Janie and I had already staked out our tent that we would be sharing together. I must have had a well-developed nesting instinct because I made a "home" out of any place I would be occupying for more than two days. Crates, appropriated from the mess tent, became cot-side end tables which we covered with grass cloth throws. A tin can holding some lush, tropical weed became our bouquet. A large five-by-eight grass cloth mat covered the bare wood floor.

We had bartered with the natives for the grass cloth trappings. We had wanted to buy the things that they produced from their cottage industry because we had thought that we would be alleviating their abject poverty by giving them some purchasing power. It was naive of us not to understand that these people could not use our money. They had no consumer goods to purchase. They needed our soap, our underwear and socks, combs, needles and thread. The most basic items were unavailable.

A young Filipino woman attached herself to us in the hope that she could swap her labor in return for consumer goods. Her name was Anacita Hipana. Anacita was so very young, still in her teens, and she had a little boy to support.

Despite her poverty, I remember her as cheerful, loyal, honest and industrious. For many of the natives, honesty was an impediment to their struggle for survival, but not so for Anacita. She remained true to herself and endeared herself to all of us. After I had left the station, Anacita corresponded with my parents in letters full of affection.

One of Anacita's chores was scrubbing our clothes which, in the rainy season, became an exercise in futility. Nothing was ever completely dry. Our clothing was always clammy. All leather goods - shoes, belts, watch bands, wallets, leather cases and holsters - were covered with a green mold. When shirts and slack waistbands became soaked with atabrine-stained perspiration, they never air-dried. The wearer's recourse was to return to his tent for another lesser soaked shirt. Even our stationery supplies were permanently glued together.

When first I stirred the embers of my memory, I was excited by the spitting sparks that teased me with the promise of greater revelations. And when the sparks ignited the flames that licked at the edges of total recall, burning away the mental blocks that barred access, I knew I was being awarded a second chance to revisit my past. But as the flames spread and threatened to engulf me, my conscience was scorched by truths and subtle shadings of those long ago happenings. The years have allowed me an objectivity and a wisdom gleaned from a life viewed from a different perspective. As I try to quench any lingering guilt and regret, I know that some things would be handled differently today.

Had I had the insight to understand the reason for Anacita's campaign, I, assuredly, would have pursued a different tack. Her letters were full of love pronouncements usually reserved for one's family. Only now, reading between the lines, I realize that she was praying for someone to be her American sponsor. She may have attempted the same approach with other service personnel. I would not have blamed her. Her country offered a barren future for her and her child, and her maternal instincts gave her the courage to beseech strangers for the promise of America. In my musings about how things might have been, I know that my parents, who would have taken on the whole world if it were possible, would have welcomed Anacita into their home and their hearts, and I would have been an enthusiastic partner. I hope that someone, more insightful than I, saw her potential and gave her that chance for a better life.

During the rainy season, the sky would open up, and abruptly dump out torrents, as if the ocean had traded places with the sky and the waves were falling from above. At those times, if I was not on duty, I would rush out of my tent, shampoo bottle at the ready, and suds up my hair. The volume of rain water was much greater than that of our feeble shower. The operation of nature's salon had one major glitch. The sky spigot would shut off as abruptly as it had opened, and I would be left, with lathered hair, standing in the middle of the compound without so much as the tapering off sprinkles of a respectable shower. With my feet ankle deep in road mud, I would find myself in an instant sauna as hot steam rose from all the jungle vegetation and the road.

Along with the deluges, were the threats of typhoons. No one was complacent when one was predicted to hit our position. At those times, the natives would scramble up the coconut trees and cut out all the coconuts. A coconut tree can attain a height of one hundred feet. The top is crowned by ten to twenty foot leaves. Nestled close to the base of the leaves are the fruits in various stages of developement, from the spathes or bracts, the white and yellow flowers that emerge from them, to the fully developed nuts. One tree can yield one hundred coconuts in a season. In a typhoon, the nuts became dangerous missiles dislodged by the ferocious winds and hurtled to the ground. I marveled as I watched the natives, running vertically on all fours, reach the treetops with uncommon speed.

We were little more than ten degrees north of the equator. The heat and humidity were conducive to causing many tropical skin diseases, most of which resisted healing in the environment in which they were spawned. Usually, a soldier was sent home if he contracted a resistant skin disease.

It was an easy ticket out because the ailment often was cured spontaneously in the cooler, dryer climate of America. Tropical skin diseases were an urgent concern of my father's. He was right on target, because later on, I fell victim to a tropical impetigo which was to cause me many uneasy minutes.

Life in Leyte was not good.....but not bad.....better for us than for the natives. There was a pervasive indolence about the place. The hot, heavy, moisture-laden air made for a listlessness. Life was unproductive. There was nothing in my immediate surroundings except our hospital and its auxiliary facilities plunked down in the jungle. I tried to imagine the vicious air, sea and land battle that raged for the liberation of Leyte.

We performed our duties with impaired efficiency, contending with a climate induced lethargy. Struggling to vanquish my inertia, I sought some motivation to force myself into action. To that end, I wandered over to the dental tent. It was a good choice. I had thirteen cavities. The dentist had a generator in his tent to power his equipment. The tools and methods were crude by today's standards, but my dental repair kept both of us busy for several sessions.

The officers' club was another welcome distraction. The front of the club had been built on solid ground, but the rest of the club was built on stilts and spanned "Schisto" creek. We had named every creek, pond, stream, any inland body of water "Schisto" because tropical waters were infested with the Schistosome, a parasitic blood fluke that caused the disease, Schistosomiasis. Our soldiers, who during the course of the fighting had to wade through one of these bodies of water, fell prey to the parasite. It is one of the most important and detrimental diseases of the tropics.

The club had bamboo poles holding up a grass roof, and a bamboo railing running around the perimeter so that no one would fall into "Schisto" creek when he was in his cups. Every evening, anyone not on duty could be found at the officers' club taking full advantage of his beer and liquor rations.

It seems that officers were entitled to an alcohol ration, and it was in Leyte that I got my first perk, a whole case of beer and liquor. I shoved the case under my cot, but it didn't take long for the others to get designs on an untapped case. They had seen me night after night at the club with an empty glass. I had determined that I would go on a psychological jag, and as the others got happier, I got happier too. It was surprising how much fun I could have by willing it so. My only alternative would have been to stay alone in my tent.

The climax of the evening never deviated. The assembled company, now fairly anesthetized, formed a large circle and did a raucous rendition of the "Hokey-Pokey". It was my first introduction to the ritual. I remember one little, short, plump doctor whose roly-poly "tummy" was most aptly suited to the part when:

> "You put your stomach in,
> You put your stomach out,
> You put your stomach in
> and you shake it all about.
> You do the Hokey-Pokey
> and you turn yourself around,
> That's what it's all about."

The evening was topped off by heaving all the chairs over the railing into "Schisto" creek. The nightly bashes at the officers' club served the purpose of excising a number of hours from the tedium of our days.

I became the most popular girl in camp with everyone being oh so nice to me, each one hoping that he would be the recipient of my donations of beer and liquor. The excuse of some of the wheedlers was that they needed the booze for "brushing their teeth, the water being so bad, don't you know?" At first, I enjoyed the attention. With emotive pretense, they gave exaggerated reasons why they should receive my rations. Men, whom I did not know or had not seen around our camp, surfaced in the hopes they might benefit from the distribution of the cache. It was all in fun - for a while - but the attention that my alcohol ration had brought me began to wear thin. It was not my nature to be rude, but the persistence and aggressiveness of some of my callers, not only in regards to my liquor, but also in nagging me for dates, began to annoy me. What was it that they didn't understand about the word, "No"?

There was a big, tall, athletic-looking man in our outfit whom I had seen frequently. He must have had some standing in our little community because I saw him most often in the midst of any activity. I had not met him, but I knew his name was Don. And so it happened that when the next officer appeared, confident that he was the most worthy of all to relieve me of my burden of booze and to thrill me with his presence, I blurted without premeditation, that no, I couldn't possibly because I was going steady with Don. Now Don was of formidable proportions, and any man with survival instincts would think twice before he put the move on Don's "steady". Pretty clever, eliminating a plethora of thirsty candidates by intimidation, but having solved one problem by creating another, I nearly strangled trying to reach Don before he discovered that he was going steady with a girl about whom he knew nothing.

I approached Don with trepidation. It was hard finding him alone, and I needed a one-to-one opportunity for this confession. First I introduced myself to him and explained how I had used his name with the implication that he was my steady. I concluded that he was, by no means, bound by this unauthorized use of his name, and that I was sorry if I had caused him any embarrassment now or in the future. He didn't say anything for a while. After a long pregnant pause during which I scarcely breathed, he said that, yes, it had been a clever ploy, and further, he didn't mind being my "steady" at all. Ohmygosh! Now what had I gotten myself into?

If I had met him at church, I could not have chosen one better for my steady. He had played football in college and hoped to have a professional career in the sport when this was all over. One does not usually credit football players with aestheticism, but I found him poetic, artistic, erudite, gentle and lots of fun. I thought, as a couple, we resembled "Mutt 'n Jeff", but Don christened us with the sobriquets, "Big Lug" and "Lil Runt", and the names stuck.

I declined all future alcohol rations.

After I met Don, the nightly forays on the officers' club lost their appeal. I had companionship. Leyte wasn't looking nearly so bad to me now. And then.....Janie and I went on night duty.

Janie had one half of the hospital, and I covered the other half. I had five long tents connected by a continuous boardwalk running at right angles through the center of the tents. Each tent had space for fifty cots. All of the admissions were medical patients. At one end of the boardwalk was a small quonset hut that ministered to approximately twelve post-operative surgical patients. At the entrance to each tent was a small, shabby, wooden desk and a chair illuminated by a single bare lightbulb hanging from a wire. These meager furnishings comprised the nurses' stations. The corpsmen performed the actual nursing chores, such as they were, and I spent most of the night recording pertinent data on the patient charts.

Nothing is so black as a jungle at night with the tall coconut fronds obscuring any feeble, ambient light from the sky. It was as if the whole scene was swallowed in the blackness. Anyone lurking out on the edges of the compound would be unable to discern anything save for a puny lightbulb that focused on a solitary figure at a desk. I felt totally exposed as if all sorts of goblins prowled the night. A few times, off in the distance, I heard the crackle of small arms fire, anonymous sounds, hanging suspended in a dark nether world.

Despite any skittishness I may have felt, the only things that intruded into my small circle of light were bugs. The bare bulb attracted all manner of flying things. I swatted, flailed my arms, brushed my charts, trying to get a surface free of bugs so that I could write without using "bug-blood" for ink. The patients' cots were equipped with mosquito netting, but Janie and I had no such protection. We had been instructed to tuck our pant legs into our combat boots and to keep our shirt cuffs and collar securely buttoned, thereby offering the minimal skin area to the bugs.

My night started at the first tent, and I worked my way through all five, charting as I went. Most of the patients had malaria, and most of them were Filipinos. I could not oversee all the medications because the time element involved in administering medication to two-hundred and fifty patients would carry way beyond the advised schedule, which allowed for the proper absorption of and proper interval between doses. This wasn't nursing. I had no assurance that everything was being done according to my standard of practice. I had to rely heavily on my corpsmen.

A situation existed that even the corpsmen could not monitor. No one had time to stand and watch each patient take his medicine. The Filipino patients would hold the pills under their tongues, spit them out as we moved down the ward, save them and sell them on the black market. Considering the number of patients and the number of pills per each, a goodly amount of medication went on the black market.

The part of the hospital that Janie oversaw was completely isolated from my half except for a narrow, stone path that connected the two sections. One night I decided to visit Janie to see if she was faring any better than I. Away from the glow of light at the nurse's station, I was shrouded in the blackness save for a flashlight to keep me oriented on the path. I was halfway between the two hospital sections when, suddenly, I was grabbed from behind by an unknown assailant. With an adrenalin rush and mighty upward heave of my arms, I broke through his crushing hold pinning me down and wrestled free. Blindly, I stumbled to Janie's first tent. My projected visit with Janie was lost in the breathlessness of my flight. Never, would I have been able to identify my would-be attacker, his face protected, forever, by the darkness. Of one thing I am sure. He was an American.

Our seven to seven shift concluded with giving the night report to the day nurses. At seven-thirty, Janie and I would stop at the mess tent to rehash the night over a breakfast of powdered eggs, powdered milk and ersatz coffee. The "coffee", black and strong, hot and bitter, was probably chickory. It wasn't too bad after we doctored it with powdered milk and lots of sugar, after first being careful to pick the bugs out of the sugar. Breakfast over, we hurried to our tent to grab some sleep before the heat of the day made further rest impossible.

We averaged three and a half hours a day of uneasy sleep, usually giving up and getting up at eleven AM. Since we had the nurses' compound all to ourselves in the day time, we would strip down to our panties thinking we would stay cooler sans clothes. One morning, a noise in our tent roused me from my stupor. Immediately alert but cautious, I slowly craned my neck to glance around the tent. There, sitting crosslegged on the floor of the tent, was a Japanese soldier. Half nude, I was loathe to spring into some ill-defined action. It was then that I spied a work crew of Japanese prisoners whacking at the jungle encroachment with scythes on the narrow strip of ground that ran behind the tents. At some distance away, at the far end of the compound, I could see a single G.I. with a rifle who was "guarding" the workers. He hadn't even missed the slacker who was hiding out in the only occupied tent in the whole compound. I was much less inclined for a confrontation as the work detail and their guard neared our tent. What to do? I rolled over on my stomach and rationalized that I was less exposed in that position. Janie, awake by now, followed suit. There we lay until they all trooped down the line. Twice, I had discovered prisoners-of-war in my boudoir; Germans at Newton D. Baker and Japanese in Leyte. Both occasions involved night duty and work details. A girl could get superstitious from these seemingly unrelated happenstances.

With our hospital duty scheduled at night, and with so few daytime hours devoted to sleep, our days were free to amuse ourselves. The possibilities were meager in Leyte. There was no library. There was no theater. Inasmuch as we had to be on duty at seven, it was too early for the nightly festivities at the officers' club. The only bright spot in this dismal picture was a beautiful stretch of beach. It was maintained by the personnel stationed on Leyte. The jungle side was fenced off and guarded. The beach itself was patrolled until closing time after dark. Generally, we could find someone off duty who could take us there. All the inland waters were unsafe for swimming, but this was the ocean, and it was bright and blue and inviting.

At what point I had included a bathing suit in my gear, I cannot say. I had donned it once in Luzon. It was hideous. It was yellow in the front, the color of my atabrine tinged skin, and a faded navy in back which made my complexion more sallow. Couple that with the fact that my only shoes were combat boots, and the sand was too hot to trod barefoot. Put a slash of red on my lips, and you have the image of a yellow girl in a yellow bathing suit striding along the beach in combat boots, looking as if she was bleeding from the lips. However, looking freakish never deterred me from availing myself of the tropical paradise that was the beach.

Navy boats routinely patrolled the shoreline of the island. I was a strong swimmer, and if I got the chance, I would swim out to one of the patrol boats when it passed our beach on its rounds. The sailors would throw me a life buoy and haul me aboard. There, I would sun on the deck, drinking soda pop, until the boat was opposite the beach on its return trip, whereupon I would dive overboard and swim to shore. The boat was not authorized to take hitchhikers, and my behavior was too audacious to be condoned. Certainly, it was unnecessary for me to create further adventures in my present circumstances. Earnestly, I told myself that I would curtail such juvenile impulsiveness. I did not always succeed.

And then there was Clancy, a friend dating back to my student days when he was a resident at Akron City Hospital.

Clenie had seen Clancy at the hospital in Leyte where she and Janie and the others had been taken when they were removed from the U.S.S. Marigold. When Clenie and I were reunited at the monastery in Luzon, she told me that she had had long conversations with Clancy, and how much it had meant to him to see someone from home.

So it was that, upon my arrival in Leyte, I inquired about the location of Clancy's hospital, and visited him at my first opportunity. I was shocked when I saw him. I remembered him as a tall, blond Swede with light blue eyes. He was very yellow from the atabrine. His balding pate was yellow too with thin little blond tendrils pulled across it. What I didn't see bothered me more than the obvious fatigue lines in his face or the way his sad eyes lit up momentarily when he saw me. Leyte had been hard on him. He was overly cautious and overly concerned about me. He had always been earnest and conscientious in his practice of medicine, but now, his demeanor bordered on fussiness. He was my peer, but he had left any youthful giddiness behind. It was hard to be buoyant in a place like Leyte, and I don't know how long he had been contending with hardships without the morale boosters of the likes of Clenie and me.

His hospital accepted female patients. If any one of us became ill, we were transplanted to his facility. I kept a tenuous grip on the temporary "homes" I had established from duty station to duty station and on the security of my peers. I would be loathe to be plucked from my outfit and sent to an unfamiliar place. Therefore, when I discovered some revolting looking vesicles on my chest and shoulders, I concealed them under my clothing and told no one....... except Clancy.

I was exhibiting one of the dreaded tropical skin diseases, tropical impetigo. It resembled the impetigo with which I was familiar, most often seen in children with vesicles around the mouth and nostrils. My condition was more savage in appearance and spread more rapidly. I refused to consider the unthinkable, that of reporting it, being admitted to that other hospital, and probably be sent home. What an ignoble end to my service career that would be! Of course, the disease curtailed my swimming since my intent was to hide it.

Clancy arranged for me to meet him in his clinic every day, and he would aid and abet me in my concealment plot. He bore a look of awful consternation on his face every morning when he hurried into the clinic. He seemed to be taking this harder than I was. If I met with success allowing me to stay with my outfit, grand! If not - about some things, one must be fatalistic.

Under sterile conditions, Clancy would lance the pustules with exquisite care to contain the exudate on sterile cotton lest it contaminate healthy skin. Despite the daily containment procedure, the ugly stuff was spreading. Soon, it would be visible. Insidiously, it was crawling up my neck above my collar line. Without an alternate strategy, I would have to report to sick call.

It was late October, 1945. The Occupation Forces had been in Japan almost two months. Lt. General Robert L. Eichelberger was commander of the Eighth Army in Japan. My uniform bore the Eighth Army patch. It was anticipated that General Eichelberger would send word to Leyte to "get those nurses up here". It was on October 28, 1945 that we got our orders for Japan.

No time! Never enough time! I did not get to say my goodbyes to Clancy. I would never become accustomed to treating my friends like expendable "throwaways". I had used him, compromised his ethics by accepting his clandestine treatments, had not given him enough one-on-one friendship time, and now, I was simply going to vanish. I don't know why I thought I was God's emissary sent to help everybody, but I did. It preyed on my mind that I had not completed my mission. And my concern for Clancy had made him my mission.

I only recall crying twice while in service. I was not too predisposed to tears, but I cried for my patients at Newton D. Baker, and I cried when I realized I would lose Don, my "steady", my big bodyguard and my friend. I had been giving chunks of my heart away every time I moved on. I had a big and generous heart, but surely, one day it would break if I continued to whittle away on it. The last time I saw Don, I spent the occasion sobbing into his shoulder. Poor Don, the "Big Lug" hadn't a clue what to do with me.

The next morning, the two and half ton troop truck came down the dusty road of our compound. The following scenario was like a television rerun. As usual, the truck was pulling out with me sprinting after it, loudly encouraged by my comrades yelling, "Come on, Miller! Come on, Miller!"

It was on such occasions as this that my lie to the GYN doctor at the time of my initial physical was most apparent and distressing. Yes, I did suffer from severe cramping every time we moved. Janie joined me in this malady. Once positioned on the hard wood bench in the truck and being smacked on the seat like riding a rough-gaited horse every time the truck lurched through a shell hole, Janie and I would dig our elbows deep into our abdomens as if we were trying to hold our internal viscera together. Or perhaps, we sought to use our elbows as a counter-irritant. The whole condition and our prescription for it struck us as so bizarre that we dissolved into laughter. I can still see Janie with such spasms of laughter that she couldn't catch her breath and with tears streaming down her cheeks because she hurt so much. In such a manner, we endured until our arrival at the 118th General Hospital. Our orders had placed us on tdy (temporary duty) at this hospital, but for billeting purposes only until flights could be arranged.

We lingered at the 118th for four days, not being permitted to leave the area because our plane would be available "momentarily". On November 2, 1945, two planes were waiting on the runway. They were Douglas-Cargo, probably DC4's or 5's. They were old and creaky so it was disconcerting when our sunset flights were delayed because of mechanical flaws. We sat on our duffel bags under the wings of the airplanes while the mechanics worked to make the planes airworthy. We lost the sunset take off; the black jungle night dropped over us; hour after hour crept by. It did not inspire confidence when, finally at 0300 (three A.M.), we boarded the plane. We would fly over open sea to our first refueling stop in Okinawa en route to a new land, a different climate, an alien people with customs and physical characteristics foreign to us.

There is name recognition for Oahu and Midway of the Hawaiian Islands; Tarawa in the Gilbert Islands; Kwajalean and Eniwetok of the Marshalls; Guadalcanal and Bougainville in the Solomons; Saipan, Tinian and Guam of the Marianas; Iwo Jima and Okinawa. These names and many more represent the valor and tenacity of our soldiers as they fought for a toe-hold on the rock and sand and jungle of these pitiful pieces of real estate in the vast Pacific. They faced a formidable foe, but counted among the casualties must be the recognition of the thousands felled by diseases prevalent in the tropics, and 131,028 more lost from war crimes including murder, torture and starvation. My move to Japan became very personal when I considered the groundwork laid, at appalling cost to our young men, that had led me and my comrades to this night flight into the enigma that was Japan.

We sat on benches that stretched the length of both sides of the plane's fuselage. The curved contour of the body prevented me from sitting erect. I draped myself on top of a long heap of val-packs and duffel hags that were piled in the center aisle the length of the plane. There I slept until the first rays of dawn crept over the horizon and into the plane's windows. We had a soldier steward who was crouched, Filipino style, on the floor making breakfast. He had a can of "sterno", denatured alcohol and wax, on which he was brewing a pot of something hot. We had not eaten since our noon meal of the previous day so the K-rations and hot drink were welcome.

It was a long flight. We touched down at Okinawa in midafternoon for food and refueling. When we disembarked, we saw, parked next to us, the most enormous plane we had ever seen. It was a B-29 Superfortress. There are planes today that dwarf the B-29, but at that time, it was a colossus. It was the Superfortress that had delivered the atomic bombs over Hiroshima and Nagasaki a scant three months past. After its capture from the Japanese, Okinawa became the base for the Superfortresses. The annals of war tell about two hundred to three hundred Superfortresses that rained devastation on the Japanese cities of Tokyo, Nagoya, Osaka, and Kobe, the last two being famous as the cultural centers of Japan. I vaguely remember scuttlebutt about these raids, but coming face to face with one of the behemoths was both sobering and provocative. Its crew invited us to take a tour from cockpit to tail. The interior was cramped. It was so full of equipment that crawling on hands and knees through openings scarcely large enough to admit a man were the only access to many areas. Once in one's area, there was no free movement throughout the fuselage. I appreciated the opportunity to inspect this historic plane.

All military installations are accustomed to providing for transients. In my experience, I do not know of any host or hostess who, with equanimity, could accept forty-two extra people who just happened to drop in for dinner and overnight lodgings, but feeding us and finding sleeping quarters for us was routine. It was too early for bed so we planned to explore the base. Abruptly, the generator failed and we were plunged into blackness. The lack of orientation to an unfamiliar place and the confusion that followed the blackout curtailed our sightseeing. Actually, being forced to retire early was exactly. what we needed, and benefiting from extra sack time stood us in good stead for the next leg of our journey

And what of my souvenir of the islands, tropical impetigo? I took it to Japan with me.

Anacita Hipana with Meredith in front of her and Janie's tent.

JAPAN

"East is East"

"East is east,
and west is west,
and never the twain shall meet."

That adage along with my early geography books that pictured cherry blossoms, kimonos, parasols and pagodas were the sum of my knowledge of the mysterious Orient. Remember as children, we believed we could tunnel to China on the other side of the world? Japan was on the opposite side of the globe, too, with her customs diametrically opposed to ours. Consider these: snorkling and slurping at meals would be odious at our dining tables, but noisy gastronomy and loud acid eructations showed appreciation for the meal in this exotic land. We enjoy privacy in the bath. The men and women of Japan are accustomed to communal baths. When relieving themselves, they opted for the side of the road when more suitable facilities were unavailable while we contrived for privacy in our toilet. Further, we have an informality in our social deportment among the sexes. Contrarily, their casualness in the bath was contradicted by their rigid social code between men and women. The disparity between our cultures gave credence to "and never the twain shall meet". There was much I would have to learn.

Playing the role of conqueror was an alien concept to me. Historically, conquering armies fought with the lusty anticipation of the promised spoils of war. With nods of approval from their generals, conquerors not only overcame their foes on the field of battle, but overran the land, burning, raping, and plundering. The vanquished always knew their fate. Understandably, the Japanese people feared that the occupation by the Americans would bring a new terror heaped on top of the terror that had rained from the skies when their cities were bombed.

Their own soldiers had raped Manchuria in China when they provoked the Mukden Incident on September 18, 1931. Japan exploited Manchuria's rich resources and cheap labor and ravished the people in an occupation that lasted into the forties, until Japan's defeat in 1945. Their managed news did not divulge any of this treachery that would bring dishonor to the nation. In the same manner, it is unlikely that the Japanese people were aware of the brutal German occupation of Europe. Nevertheless, American prisoners can testify to the brutality of their captors, including women who were forced to service the Japanese soldier.

It was with no small amount of pride in my country to note America's policy of reconstruction, humanitarianism and lawful government in its occupation of Japan and Germany. Japanese, German and Italian prisoners-of-war were treated justly and humanely. It is a tribute to America's greatness that she did not succumb to vengeance and refrained from giving back, in kind, to her former enemy the harsh treatment perpetrated on our people held captive by the Japanese and German military.

Another concept that I found troublesome was that of hatred. Was I being disloyal if I did not hate the enemy? Should I not hold resentment, bitterness and contempt in my heart? Perhaps I had a congenital flaw in my "hate" gene because I found it so enervating to use my strength on hate that I ceased attempting it.

Besides, I rather liked the people, particularly the little Japanese girls. After their initial fright of the Americans, the people relaxed, and as was their wont, became cooperative with the new regime. By nature or design, they were accustomed to following orders and seemed more comfortable with someone at the helm - albeit an American.

My first view of Japan was seeing the majesty of Mt Fujiyama, its perfect cone rising through the mists that girdled it about half way from its summit. It seemed detached from anything earthly as it rode the cushion of clouds beneath it, showing off all aspects of itself as the plane approached, flew briefly beside it and turned to circle it. Its reality was more beautiful than any stylized silk print or watercolor. The steward opened the wide door of the plane so that we might view "Fuji" unobstructed. Our plane's air speed was not sufficient to create a suction at the open door, and our pilot gave us time for picture taking. I would save that image in my memory and would call upon it many times when the destruction and poverty in Japan palled on me.

Our plane landed at Atsuki airfield near Yokohama in early afternoon. Then followed a classic example of the principle of "hurry-up-and-wait".

Had we not, with some urgency, been summoned to Japan? Why was there no one to meet us? In all of officialdom, there was nobody of authority to whom we could present ourselves. The airport continued with its normal operation bringing planes in and sending planes out while we sat under the wings of our plane out on a runway. Unlike commercial travel today where the planes taxi up to a covered walk-way, we were parked at the far reaches of the airstrip.

The afternoon was waning, and a brisk wind had sprung up bringing a chill with it. We were clad in our suntans and unprepared for November temperatures. We had left the tropics for the temperate zone two days before, and had not become acclimated to cooler temperatures. The Yokohama area lay between 35 and 36 degrees north latitude with temperatures similar to Tennessee. While we waited, I discovered a dramatic change.

Different ones of the girls would go on scouting details. Two of us headed across the airfield toward some small buildings in the distance looking for a bathroom. While there, I made my discovery. My disease had continued to spread rapidly, involving my neck, chest, axillae, shoulders and back. Now I was miraculously free of tropical impetigo. The only vestiges remaining were little red dots and scabs resembling the tag end of chickenpox. I was so relieved that I was euphoric. I had not recognized the extent of my anxiety concerning my affliction. A single day of cool temperature had triggered a cure.

At one end of the airport were rows of substantial looking buildings. Originally, they had been occupied by the Japanese air force school. Now they housed a wing of the American Air Force. Word of the plight of the stranded nurses circulated quickly. Before dusk closed in on us, we watched with curiosity, as a large group of Air Force men hurried across the runways toward us. When they neared our group, we saw that they were carrying what looked like clothing. Soon, each one of us was "adopted" by one of them, and the clothing they brought, flight jackets, scarves and gloves, was on our person. I had been adopted by "Joel". I was swathed in his big flight jacket, and along with the rest, I was taken to a large mess hall on the base. We had had one nutritious meal in over two days, supper at Okinawa, but now we would eat our fill from a menu that was far from the powdered, reconstituted fare on Leyte.

By nightfall, billeting had been found at an installation formerly occupied by Japanese soldiers.

The 128th Station Hospital

Too tired to care, we waited until morning to investigate our surroundings. We had been assigned to the 128th Station Hospital for rations and billeting. Two days later on November 6, 1945, we were placed on tdy at the 128th. The familiar layout, consisting of long, narrow buildings bisected by walks, resembled other installations with any differences being found in construction materials. Newton D. Baker was brick; the 117th was canvas; the 128th was wood gone shabby with peeling white paint. Our quarters were in the last, narrow building, a barracks that had been partitioned off into small cubicles. Each held two cots with a tiny aisle in between. Each room had a little radiator, most of which were inoperable. Janie and I shared an icy room.

Early on at the 128th, we were inoculated with flu shots. Janie had a violent reaction with chills so extreme that they resembled malaria. I piled our trench coats, the air force jackets and finally myself on top of her trying to warm her in that frigid room. Thankfully, her symptoms ameliorated without further complications.

I decided that I would brave the Japanese shower. Now, their showers had all sorts of dials and gauges and faucets and unexpected water jets. If you turned something, you had no advance warning what you might have activated. It would take one knowledgeable of an airplane cockpit to decipher the intricacies of a Japanese shower. The shower room was as bitter cold as outdoors. Standing there, turning blue, I tentatively reached for one of the faucets. Immediately I was blasted with freezing cold water jets that felt like hundreds of hypodermic needles. Frantically, I fumbled for the faucet to turn it off before I crystallized, when I hit something that inundated me with near-scalding water that poured out of a circular tubular affair above my head. I grabbed my towel and ran, vowing never to take another shower as long as I was in Japan. By golly! I would wear my khaki "long-johns" and long-sleeved undershirt and wash only the skin that showed!

The 128th bore a similarity to the 117th in Leyte in that it had ward after ward of malaria. The disease is caused by one of a variety of protozoa, the Haematozoa Malariae, which is transmitted by the anopheles mosquito. The soldiers brought their malaria with them when they were transferred from the tropics to Japan for the occupation. The characteristic chills, fever and sweats varied in duration and severity depending on the type of malaria parasite involved. Complications often involved other organ systems. We ministered to some mighty sick boys.

The wards were heated by pot-belly stoves, but the rest of the hospital, halls, nurses stations, and auxiliary rooms were cold. As a result, we appeared on duty lacking anything resembling regulation garb. Ragtag described our attire, with sweaters, jackets and coats garnered from our male friends, anything to keep warm.

Early in the occupation, it had come to pass that the brass in Tokyo wanted the U.S. army to go "stateside" at once which meant that everyone must present himself or herself in class "A" uniform at all times. For us, that meant seersucker wrap-arounds on floor duty and dress uniforms on all other occasions. The hospital was too cold for the former, and our woolen dress uniforms were not in our possession having been sent home before duty in the tropics. To confuse the dilemma further, our chief nurse was being hassled by her superiors to get those women into proper uniform. She, in turn, ordered us into acceptable dress. We continued to wear our unique get-ups; our chief continued to fume in frustration. She had to have realized that we could not conform to the uniform dictum inasmuch as seersuckers were inadequate and we didn't have any class "A's" to wear.

The uniform controversy persisted. A group of us had the opportunity to go into Tokyo. Postwar Tokyo had not recovered, and there would not be much to see or do, but any reason to get off the base - or, in our case, the hospital - was sufficient. I'll admit that we did look peculiar in our suntans, combat boots, covered almost to our knees by oversized flight jackets. We were made all the more comical by large gloves enlongating our fingers so that we resembled gorillas swinging along. I had wound Joel's scarf around my head like a turban, not exactly regulation head gear. Once in Tokyo, we became acutely aware of our appearance. Our "just off the farm" look was up against the polished image of bright, young officers, in class "A's" with shiny insignia, hastening hither and yon looking important. We were trying to look nonchalant, but before we could initiate some plan of action, we were nabbed. The M.P.'s. (military police) arrested us for being out of uniform. I almost laughed. Imagine not having anything better to do than to seize a group of girls out sightseeing! The M.P.'s didn't have a prayer when they found themselves surrounded by a bunch of females, all talking at once, like hens in the hen house when the fox tried to get in. The M.P.'s. were thoroughly flustered by the time they finally were made to understand that we didn't have any proper uniforms to wear.

Joel must have been ashamed to be seen with me looking so tacky in his hand-me-downs because one day he took me into Yokohama to a Japanese tailor. He had not told me the reason for our trip into town so I had misgivings when the jeep stopped in front of a shabby, rundown warehouse. We ascended steep, dark stairs worn thin by the tread of generations of feet. The top of the stairs opened into a long, shadowy room totally unadorned of anything to relieve its starkness. The room was being used as a barracks for enlisted men. The ugly room contributed to a listlessness in the several G.I.'s who were flopped on their cots. At the end of the dark room was a door that led into a small closet-like space. Waiting for us was a Japanese tailor.

He had some green material that was not army issue, but the color was close enough to pass if one did not scrutinize it. He measured me for a skirt. Then he measured me for an Eisenhower-style jacket that he would cut down from an enlisted man's uniform.

When I was decked out in my green skirt and Eisenhower jacket, I was as proud as if I had a new party dress, and I looked much more presentable even though neither garment was government issue.

It was many weeks before dress uniforms arrived from the States. Meanwhile, we at the 128th were an embarrassment to our superiors.

For many, many years, I had a recurrent dream about the old warehouse. In my dream, I am hidden in the shadows of the room. Into the room, in single file, came everybody I had ever known. The order in which they paraded by was chronological beginning with elementary school, progressing through high school, college, nurses training and so on. Each group was dressed as it would have been at the time I knew them. I loved the dream because, in it, I renewed friendships with people I had forgotten, with friends who had died or moved away, with grandparents long gone, with everyone who had passed by on his or her journey. The dream stopped abruptly. I have kept hoping that it would resurface again one day.

One morning, I was hurrying along the wooden walk from my barracks as the little Japanese housemaids were coming from the opposite direction. They minced along with small running steps, smiling and bowing as they approached. As each neared me, she would nod and sing, "Ohio!", "Ohio!". I beamed back, delighted, and thinking, "How very sweet of them. They went to all the trouble to learn what state in America I was from." It was with chagrin that I learned that "Ohio" is a greeting like, "Hello."

Another time, I had forgotten something in my room and returned to retrieve it. I opened the door on five very startled and frightened little maids. I estimated their ages to be from eight to twelve. They had gotten into my cosmetics and were helping themselves to rouge and lipstick. There stood five little, terrorstruck "clowns" with big, round blobs of rouge on their cheeks and lipstick that missed the lips' contours by a mile. I quickly pulled the door shut and leaned against the outside wall, holding my sides as I shook with silent laughter. There would be another incident involving cosmetics that pointed out the Japanese womens' love of facial adornment.

It was nice having Joel for an escort. We had settled into a more stable routine. We were still subject to sudden moves and upheavals, but the semi-permanence of the 128th was a welcome respite. The Air Force men would take us to their officers' club in the evening for music and dancing. They had made the club from one of the existing barracks. Using civilian skills of masonry, plumbing and carpentry, they had fashioned a very presentable hangout. They had "appropriated" white table cloths, flatware and other accouterments. "Appropriate" is a service slang term for procuring necessary supplies, sometimes under questionable circumstances.

Joel was much more sophisticated than I. When other couples would disappear into barracks rooms, he would have liked to follow suit, but I had laid down my ground rules early in our relationship, and, with an amused tolerance, he abided by my wishes. The actions that we took, as a result of my dictates, did not endear us to the rest of the company. Being deserted by everyone, we would entertain ourselves by prowling the halls, pounding on everyone's door and yelling, "Police! Open up!" That did not make a hit.

One evening, our escorts were brimming with excitement and teased us about a surprise they had for us. They could hardly contain themselves as they led us through their officers' club to a door off a hall. With mock fanfare, they threw open the door, and there - beautiful, shining, thronelike - sat a brand-new, honest-to-goodness, American-style TOILET! It was, indeed, a wonderful surprise. We had been contending with a closet that had a hole in the floor, the typical Japanese toilet. It was an "appropriation", and we never questioned its origin.

I knew things were going too well to last....I was going to lose Janie. Word had come that all personnel over the age of thirty-five would be relieved of duty and sent home. Too soon, Janie was gone. We had said our goodbyes one night at Atsuki Airport. I was inconsolable as the plane disappeared into the midnight sky. I never saw Janie again, but we corresponded with "remember when" letters until her death in 1991.

With Janie gone, I moved into Mary Kay's room which was located at the opposite end of the hall from my room, ostensibly because her room was heated. My occupying the vacant cot was made possible because her roommate was hospitalized with hepatitis. This change of accommodations lasted one night whereupon I hied back to my cold room. Mary Kay was accustomed to bringing canned goods from the commissary to her room. On this first night, Mary Kay had pried open a can of stewed tomatoes and was slurping them directly from the can. She sat the unused portion on a wood crate by her cot. The leftover food was an invitation to critters with squatters' rights.

I had hung my valpack (a type of garment bag) on a nail at the head of my cot. It was unzipped and the opened flap fell over the top of my cot, making a convenient runway for what happened next.

We went to sleep. I awoke to scratching and running sounds. There was movement in my valpack and at the top of my cot. My long hair, festooned around my head, became involved in the scurrying activity. Paralyzed, I managed a hoarse whisper to Mary Kay. She was, delicately put, "earthy", and also unflappable. She merely groaned at being disturbed, rolled over in bed, and said, "It's those damned rats again." Even though I only stayed the one night, I like to regale my friends with the story about having rats in my hair.

I seemed to have a penchant for blowing the opportunity of any rapport with my chief nurses. Our chief at the 128th was a large, dour woman who held herself aloof from us second "Louies". Although, as a captain, she was only two ranks above us, she maintained a formality and rigidity toward us. She was always surrounded by her coterie of colonels. She had never acknowledged me except to carp about my long hair which managed to escape all my attempts at confinement.

Because of the distance that she maintained from the rest of us, it caused me much surprise when she appeared in my quarters one day. She was all smiley and ingratiating. Her demeanor of coziness and intimate familiarity did not come easy for her, and she did not pull it off well. All of this conspired to set off alarms in my head.

It seems one of her colonels had his eye on me, and he had instructed her to bring me to him. He may have been a perfectly nice man, but the whole action smelled like a procurement to me. I was offended. I could have let her down easy and saved myself harassment in the future. Instead, I drew my small frame up high - I could make myself look taller than I was - and loftily told her that I reserved the right to choose my own friends when I was off duty. Her failure to bring back the prize did not enhance her prestige with the colonel, and I had put myself in an untenable position by causing my chief embarrassment.

I got in trouble again.

This time it involved one of the medical officers. Never had I intended to be an obstructionist. It is not easy to be principled in the face of influences, temptations, threats or consequences. However, I never doubted my decisions despite the aforementioned hazards.

For some time, I had been specialing a dangerously sick boy. Memory does not serve me when I try to recall the intricacies of his case. I can say that he had some grievious insult to his gastrointestinal system. In retrospect, I think that it was probably peritonitis, an inflammation of the peritoneum, the serous membrane lining the abdominal cavity and reflecting over the internal viscera. Its cause is from the rupture of an intra-abdominal abcess, such as a ruptured appendix or a stomach rupture; taking infection directly from an inflamed adjacent organ; a direct bloodstream infection in patients with septicemia. The prognosis was grave.

I am not conversant with the mortality rate today from peritonitis. Perhaps, with the wide range of antibiotics and new technology, the occurrence of this illness is rarer, or at least, one can be more optimistic about its outcome. But, in 1945, only God and exquisite nursing care would bring my patient through. The care that I had learned to provide was a very involved, sensitive, meticulous, art. It is a lost art in this day of modern equipment and advanced medicines, but we did save patients, and I was going to save this deathly ill young man.

As the days passed, I could see almost imperceptible changes in my patient. The special nurses on the other shifts worked just as hard on him, and although he was not out of danger, we allowed ourselves some hope. The medical officer watched him closely, too, and was pleased with his progress.

The officer was the antithesis of the calm, easy going, confidence-inspiring doctor. He was a quick, impulsive, shoot-from-hip sort of man. His speech was clipped. He was volatile and given to rages.

He burst into the room on that fateful morning with the pronouncement that we were going to feed our patient. I was to go to the commissary and get eggs and milk and juice and any other liquid goop I could find. We were going to mix it all together, hook a funnel onto his lavage tube - the tube by which we cleansed his stomach - and pour the concoction in the funnel. As gently persuasive as I could be, I said that perhaps we were rushing things; that our boy wasn't quite ready for the introduction of the prescribed liquid diet. Privately, I shuddered at the potage he planned to dump into my patient, and my fear for his life was genuine.

The officer was furious that I had demurred and hadn't, at the instant the order was given, rushed off to do his bidding. He shrieked at me to go! It was at that point that I quietly told him I could not obey his order. His laser-like eyes zeroed in on me as he said (what I already knew) that disobeying a direct order was a court-martial offense, and that he would press charges.

I was in deep conflict with myself - not that I was afraid of court-martial and its far-reaching consequences. My conflict concerned disobeying an order. In civilian hospitals, it was the nurse's duty to follow the doctor's orders. Here was the same situation involving doctor and nurse with the added proviso of the entire military structure predicated on following orders down through the whole hierarchy. Without it, the military would collapse and anarchy would result.

My decision was not a frivolous one. Also, I did not enjoy the discomfort that I had caused the medical officer. Who did I think I was? What self-conceit made me think I could topple tradition and take on the establishment? But my patient came first. About that, there could be no compromise.

The officer left the room, shouting over his shoulder, that he'd do it himself and deal with me later. I calmly performed my duties repressing any personal anxiety but feeling very apprehensive about my patient.

The medical officer returned with his cocktail of nutriments. I watched, helplessly, as he hooked the funnel to the lavage tube and poured the mixture into it. I was holding my patient's hand, and I closed my eyes and silently prayed that my predictions would not come true. I could feel the boy's hand spasm as I held it. My eyes flew open, alert now, as I bent over him. His body seemed to jolt , and then lay still as he went into shock.......

The boy lived. With diligent care, we had brought him back again to his tenuous hold on life. The medical officer made himself scarce. He did not apologize for almost precipitating a disaster, but neither did he ever mention court-martial again.

The Air Force men continued to relieve us from our routine. I really needed to have someone minister to me after the psychic trauma I suffered from almost losing my patient and my career in a single blow. Joel was good at that. We visited friends at other Air Force installations; we explored little, remote villages where Americans were still an oddity; we poked around dusty little shops. At first, there were no consumer goods available. In large centers like Tokyo, one could find paper souvenirs in sidewalk stalls, but anything of value had been hidden before the Americans came. Additonally, the whole nation had been engaged in manufacturing war materiel. Imagine my delight when I discovered an objet d'art concealed in a dark corner of the farthest recesses of a tiny shop. The glass on the front of the case was opaque from years of grime. The shopkeeper seemed vexed that I had discovered it and was hesitant about showing it to me.

The object was that of an old Japanese fisherman, standing on a large rock, reeling in a big fish. His body, arms and legs and the rock were of teak. His head, hands, feet, a pouch attached to his belt, his fishing pole, fish and creel, even the bobber, were carved ivory. His tunic was carved with a floral design; his pajamas were draped on his legs, braced for balance on the rock. His hands were gnarled. Every metatarsal bone was delineated on his slim feet, and on his face was a look of senile glee. I loved him. I had to have him for my mother. He took my whole pay check, but considering that the inflation rate was one hundred yen to the dollar, I was much lighter after my purchase. Would that the reluctant shopkeeper could have known what an appreciative home was waiting for the old fisherman. He is on display in my home now.

> In defeat, Japan's economy was ruined. The instability of the yen, the lack of consumer goods, the collapse of the infra-structure and rampant inflation plunged the market into further chaos. The occupation forces arbitrarily set the rate of exchange at one hundred yen to the dollar so that the armed forces and the civilian employees could be paid. The yen continued to be unpredictable changing up or down with each gust of the market. Finally, in 1949, the occupation forces, desperate to stabilize the yen, decreed to set the rate of exchange at the value of the yen at that date, which was three hundred and sixty yen to the dollar.

One evening, Joel took me and another couple to a Japanese gentlemen's home for dinner. He must have been affluent because he had both a home and food. Upon entering any Japanese dwelling, one removed one's shoes and donned white socks before coming into the living quarters.

The home was small with one large room that could be sectioned off by sliding, opaque, window-pane partitions. The only furnishing, a low, square table graced the center of the room. Our host, who was clad in a plain black kimono, motioned for us to take our places at the table. He, and another Japanese man incidental to the dinner party, sat on one side. The other nurse and I sat opposite them with our escorts sitting on the remaining two sides opposite each other. Our positions at the table were relevant to what I would observe during the course of the meal. The Orientals seemed comfortable sitting with their knees bent in front of them, and their bodies rocked back on their heels. We were pressed to maintain that position and fidgeted between that and sitting cross-legged or with knees bent to the side. It was not customary for women to eat with the men, but we were tolerated as guests. The women of the household would eat later, depending upon the generosity of their husbands.

There was no heat save for charcoal braziers, one for each corner of the table. When one's hands became too cold to hold the chopsticks, they could be cupped around the brazier to warm them. If my nutrition depended on chopsticks, I would not be long for this world.

The meal was long with several courses. First came a clear soup with a carrot, an onion and a small potato in it. I passed on the soup. I couldn't get a potato or carrot to stay between my chopsticks, and it would have been gauche to spear a vegetable with them. Next came pieces of raw fish with little clamshell dishes of sauce. A warning from Father flashed through my mind: NEVER eat raw fish. Then came a vegetable and steamed rice medley, and on and on it went. The other girl wasn't faring any better than I was. Our escorts alternated between amusement and embarrassment. They had instructed us to create a loud belch to show appreciation, but, alas, I failed at that skill too.

Joel and the other officer had mastered a workable knowledge of the language so they carried the burden of conversation. I suppose women, like children, were to be seen but not heard so we remained discreetly quiet.

My feet were freezing in that frigid room, and I was starving because of my ineptness with chopsticks. The meal would have been a dismal failure were it not for two Japanese "mamma-sans" who peeked from behind a curtain that concealed the kitchen. Our hosts were positioned with their backs to the curtain. We girls faced the curtain and, in the ensuing pantomine, needed only to be concerned that our hosts were not looking at us as we gestured to the ladies. The two men would have been dismayed at the drama playing out behind their backs.

I don't know how I came by it, but I had polish on my nails plus a little rouge and lots of lipstick. The ladies of the kitchen would giggle quietly behind their hands and nod and smile at us. Then they pointed to their lips before pointing to me. I would touch my lips and nod and smile back. They repeated the miming with the cheeks, the hair, the nails with much giggling and appreciation, and I would respond in kind. In such a manner, we communicated. I would open my eyes wide as I showed off my nails making comical faces as I did so.

If they could have safely erupted into laughter, they would have. I delighted in them and gave them a little fun too. Their appreciation was all the more pleasing because usually, the Orientals thought Occidentals were coarse and unattractive.

It was Christmas, 1945.

It is never conducive to positive morale to steep oneself in the nostalgia of one's traditional Christmas at home; to close one's eyes and see in heart and mind exactly what was transpiring now; trimming the tree, wrapping presents, helping Mother with the cookies, caroling parties. I was here, in Japan, and I was going to make Christmas......for somebody.

Joel was Jewish and I was Christian. No matter. I would make Christmas for Joel. I became very excited making my preparations. It was a selfish pursuit because I was having a wonderful time making a surprise box.

I dyed roller bandages with merthiolate and gentian violet for red and blue ribbon. I decorated paper towels for wrapping paper. I secured a large cardboard carton and decorated it with a big snowman and snowflakes fashioned from surgical cotton. I cut out eyes and buttons of "coal" and twig arms from paper that I had inked black and pasted them on the snowman. Then I gathered bottles of aspirin and vitamins, band-aids, boxes of sterile dressings, burn ointment all wrapped individually and tied with my dyed roller bandage. I added shaving equipment, combs, miscellaneous toilet articles and canned fruits from the kitchen. I filled the box. It looked surprisingly festive.

I was like a little kid waiting to present my gift to Joel on Christmas Eve. He was so touched by the gesture that he cried, and I cried too. Making that box is the only memory I have of Christmas 1945, but you know? It was one of the best Christmases I ever had.

I was involved in my annual New Year's Eve accident when our jeep slid off the road into a ditch on the way to the officers' club. Not long after, my little world that I had carved out at the 128th fell apart.

Betrayal, hurt, disappointment, fury - all of these.

Joel had come to me with a solemnity I had not seen in him before. He had always been so urbane and debonair. Now, he was uncertain and troubled. He told me he was in love with me and needed to overcome some obstacle that stood in the way of our future. My stomach flip-flopped. I knew we were fond of each other, that we filled a void in each other's lives with companionship in the strange, transitory circumstances in which we found ourselves, but Joel's worldliness had always seemed to preclude permanency. My spinning mind was already considering the ramifications of his declaration when he dropped his bombshell. In essence, this is what he said, "I'm married. I have a wife and a baby daughter I have never seen. I stopped writing to my wife weeks ago. I don't want to go home to her. I want a divorce, and I want to make my life with you." I wish I could have had the "vapors and swooned away". Instead, his words ricocheted around my brain as I tried to make sense of the torrent of emotions that were tumbling around like marbles in a lotto cage.

Yes, I was hurt because I admitted to a kind of love for him. I was awash in my disappointment because I virtually had put my life in his hands, and he had taken care of me and made me feel secure. I had admired him and had elevated him in esteem. Foolishly, I should have remembered that we all have feet of clay. Betrayal pushed to the fore, but his betrayal of me was nothing compared to his betrayal of his wife. Then came my fury. Fury is almost a stranger to me. The fingers of one hand number more than the times fury has taken possession of me.

Anyone who has seen me in action on the very few occasions when I have been furious will testify that no one has been dressed down until he has been dressed down by me. And so, Joel got the full force of my tirade. He was ordered to write loving letters to his wife, send presents and pictures of Daddy to his baby danghter. I figuratively boxed his ears and marched him to the nearest town that featured Japanese pearls and helped him pick out the best and most expensive pearls in town. He was told to buy silks and lacquer ware and anything else available in this country that was only now beginning to stock its empty shelves.

Joel followed me around like a puppy with its tail between its legs as I swooped around like an avenging angel buying presents for his wife. His acute embarrassment waned as he got into the spirit of our shopping spree. It had the affect of turning his mind in the right direction as he pondered his choices - home. Also, he saw another facet of the woman to whom he had avowed his love only a few short days ago. No doubt, he was learning how lucky he was that the Fates[19] would spare him from a life with this Harpy.[20]

I was drained when my rage was spent, and I was very lonely. I missed Joel terribly, but it was my devout hope that he returned to his wife and baby daughter and "lived happily ever after."

We received our orders to vacate the 128th and move into Yokohama.

Don was transferred to Yokohama from Leyte.

*Meredith, sporting her Eisenhower jacket, with
one of the little Japanese house maids.*

After many weeks, our class "A,s", arrived from the states. We had been an embarrassment to our superiors.

The 334th Station Hospital

At last, I would join my assigned unit, the 334th Station Hospital. Recently, through the help of a former member of the 334th, Myrl Jean Hughes, physical therapist, I have come into possession of a history of the unit. For many years, I have been curious about the hospital to which I was attached, albeit in name only.

The five hundred bed 334th Station Hospital was activated, as a complete hospital entity, on August 15, 1943 at Camp Ellis, Illinois. The unit departed Camp Ellis on January 18, 1944 and arrived in Milne Bay, New Guinea on February 19, 1944. Leaving the Milne Bay staging area in July 1944 for Hollandia, New Guinea, the hospital began operating as a unit and served with distinction until it ceased operations at that location on September 30, 1945. In addition to providing the medical and surgical needs of the area, the 334th had, among its patients, repatriated prisoners who had been captives of the Japanese for three years, large numbers of patients from hospital ships and army transports, and battle casualties from the Philippines.

I thought it might be interesting to correlate some dates of "my" unit with some of my activities:

July 13, 1945-The 334th was receiving an award for distinguished service.

I was in the middle of the Pacific Ocean.

Aug. 15, 1945-The unit had completed two years service since its activation at Camp Ellis, Illinois.

I was billeted at an old Jesuit monastery in the hills of Luzon waiting for tdy orders.

Sept. 30, 1945-The 334th had ceased operations in New Guinea and was at a staging area waiting for movement orders to a forward area.

I had been transferred to Leyte and was working at the 117th Station Hospital.

Oct. 24, 1945-Twenty-four army nurses, one hospital dietician, and one physical therapist were flown to Leyte and billeted at the 118th to await transportation home.

Oct. 28, 1945-I was at the 118th, along with twenty-eight army nurses, one hospital dietician, one physical therapist, for billeting and rations awaiting transportation to Japan.

Without knowledge of each others' presence, we were, in effect, having a "changing of the guard" as we replacements were proceeding to Japan to take up our duties with the 334th.

The rest of the organization, the medical staff and enlisted personnel, moved to Yokohama, December 7, 1945, four years after Pearl Harbor on December 7, 1941. They took up duties at the 43rd Field Hospital in the Ohteri Primary School building in south Yokohama. This was the schoolhouse of my story.

The combined complement of the 334th and the 43rd overwhelmed the small facility and there ensued much readjustment with transfers, reassignments, and personnel returning home. The resulting distillation of the 334th and the 43rd operated the hospital limited by inadequate laboratory facilities, inactive dental department, and handicapped surgical service, due to experienced technicians homeward-bound under the point system. Such were the conditions when I take up my story at the schoolhouse,.

First, however, those of us who had flown from Leyte to Japan in early November would vacate the 128th Station Hospital and join the personnel from the 334th/43rd in establishing a hospital in downtown Yokohama.

Also, we would experience a surprising variation in the usual army billeting practices.

After months of roughing it in less than comfortable surroundings, our new accommodations were luxurious beyond anything the army could conceive. It must have been a mistake. The army wouldn't have knowingly billeted us in a mansion, would they? They had lodged us in the former Belgium Embassy. The embassy was a mansion built on a bluff high above Yokohama on "Embassy Row", a long row of "chocolate houses" hidden snugly behind high white walls. They were strangely undisturbed by the bombings and destruction elsewhere in Yokohama.

> As a child, when on outings with my parents, our route would sometimes take us through an upscale neighborhood. It was in relation to the homes there that I first heard the adjective "rich" applied to anything other than chocolate. Thereafter, it had seemed logical to me to call all large homes "chocolate houses" .

A gate in the wall led to an inner court. There was a guard house at the entrance and space for jeeps that would ferry us to and from the hospital. The massive door of the mansion fed into a large foyer of pink marble. A broad marble staircase with heavy marble newel posts, wide bannisters and turned balusters ascended to the second floor. Upstairs were six bedrooms divided into two groups of three, each group served by a large marble bathroom. In addition to one of those torturous Japanese showers designed to confound the unsuspecting, was a tub! A bathtub! I had not seen a bathtub since I had left home. There are two kinds of people: shower people and tub people. I am a tub person. The height of ecstasy is to lie down in a tub full to the top with soothing warm water, then to lean your head against the cool rim of the tub and let all your cares slide away. Realistically, that would be unlikely since I would be sharing the bathrooms with all the other girls.

Four of us shared a bedroom. We had graduated to metal cots with springs and thin little mattresses. Mary Kay occupied the bunk on my right. That fact would be important and aggravating later on.

It was in the bedroom that we experienced our first of many earthquakes. We had retired. A rattling and shaking alerted us. We all chorused at once, "What's happening?" Our metal bunks began dancing across the floor like "Dodgem" cars at an amusement park. It was a disorienting, dizzying sensation as if we weren't certain whether or not we were imagining something. It passed almost as soon as it had begun. We took the many tremors that followed in stride.

Our meals were served in a large well-appointed dining room, seated at a table large enough for all of us at one time. A mamma-san prepared our meals. She and her whole family occupied servants' quarters near the kitchen. I was poking around the back of the house and came upon them all sleeping on mats on the floor. In this war-torn country, they felt fortunate to have a warm, safe place in which to stay.

We entertained our soldier beaus in a large living room that always had a hospitable fire burning in its huge fireplace. The chief nurse used a large library, also with a fireplace, as her bedroom-sitting room. It was still winter, but I was warm for the first time since my arrival in Japan.

It was off to work setting up a new hospital and getting it ready for business.

We had moved into an abandoned department store, one of the few intact buildings in Yokohama. It was a tall, skinny building with one elevator that opened onto one large room at every floor. The first seven floors were wards. Each ward was partitioned at one end, making a small private suite for officer patients. The nurse's desk was at the other end of the ward, giving her full view of all the patients. Another partition created a small room for the doctor's office. The wards filled rapidly with accidents and postoperative patients.

The top floor, the eighth, became our surgery. It was a well-equipped, modern surgical suite, capable of major surgery. It would not have been so had our medical officers not gone out in the bay to a navy ship and returned with operating tables, flood lights, instruments, a sterilizing autoclave, materiel necessary for performing surgery.

My first assignment at the 334th was in surgery. I had not been in surgery since my student days, but some skills, though rusty, are never lost. Mary Kay was head of surgery. She may have lacked some of the graces, but she was an excellent nurse.

In every assignment, there is always one memory that won't go away; I had no sooner come on duty this day when we had an emergency. A young soldier had severed his femoral artery when his gun accidentally discharged as he was cleaning it. This was one of those stupid, careless, tragic accidents that should never have happened if he had been handling his equipment properly.

The wound was high in the groin. I was scrub nurse that day, the one that stands at the table with the surgeon slapping the instruments into his hand. We commenced at 0800. Nine hours later, the surgeon halted the operation. He was heroic in his valiant attempts to splice the severed artery and save the soldier's leg. The slippery, elusive artery defied every skill employed to join its shattered ends. Exhausted, defeated, the surgeon was heartsick at his failure. He scheduled the amputation.

This incident was the more grievious since hostilities had stopped. The battlefield wounds concomitant with war are an anticipated reality in the service medical communities, but this, this was all the more agonizing because it was so needless.

There was another trauma, this to my inner-self, one that renewed itself every day when I came on duty. From eight floors up, I could look out on a panorama of destruction. Much of the rubble had been cleared away, and immediately next to our high-rise hospital, the army construction people had erected a mess hall. All else was barren devastation. A road led away from our installation. The road crowned in the middle with a deep drainage ditch on each side. There, in the ditch, lived a family: a mother, father and two little boys. A sheet of corrugated metal spanning the ditch served as their roof.

Every morning, the mother would gather debris and build a little fire on which she heated something in an old, black coffee pot. The two little boys, each with a small bucket, would cross the street to the mess hall and scrounge in the garbage for food. The month was January with its cold and snow and rain. The ditch flooded when it rained. The winds blew unmercifully under the makeshift roof making a wind tunnel of the ditch. Not so much as ragged pieces of cloth hung over the open sides of the ditch to block the weather.

It was not enough for me to acknowledge that this family was yet another casualty of war. What was our policy ? How could I, individually, help them? Must I resign myself to their travail? I could not leave my post and go out on the street to do what I yearned to do. All my life, I had wanted to be a "Lady Bountiful"[21], but my impulses were curtailed by various restrictions. Now, I suffered from my inability to do anything to alleviate this tragedy that unfolded before my eyes every day, eight floors below.

I joined a conspiracy among the girls in surgery. Someone had adopted a little boy. He was an orphan about eight years old. He was brought to the surgery and secreted there. Our part in the conspiracy was to keep him well hidden and to smuggle food to him. Bringing food to a small boy seemed simple enough, but since it must be accomplished under the prying eyes of our C.O. (Commanding Officer), we had to do a little out-maneuvering.

He was a martinet, the first of that ilk under whom we had served. He was small and dark with intense black eyes that roved continually around a room to catch any misstep. He wanted those under his command to be inflexibly military. We women had driven him to a place he had never been, a state of "apoplexy". He would roar at us that we were first, last and always officers, then nurses and, finally women in that order. Reversing those positions, we told him, "Oh no! We are women first, then nurses and, lastly, officers." He was at his wit's end trying to manage these female civilians in uniform, and, because to him we were like disobedient children, he scarcely let us out of his sight.

It was his watchful eye in the mess hall that concerned us most if we were to smuggle food to our little boy. He had directed that a dais be built at one end of the mess hall. There he sat with his officers commanding a view of the entire room.

One at a time, each of us would return to the chow line for seconds. Since our C.O. was obsessive in his vigilance, we would make our raids on the chow line with his piercing eyes following our every move. To him, it was implausible that women, not of Amazonian proportions, could consume so much food. Every time I lifted my eyes to look in his direction, I thought he was staring at me alone. Was he suspicious? Did I have guilt written all over my face? I thought it must be so, as I surreptitiously slid morsels off my plate into the napkin on my lap. We garnered sufficient food in that manner to feed a small boy. No way would we have been permitted to shelter a child were we to have been overt in providing for him.

I was placed on night duty and transferred to one of the wards. My patients ranged in age from eighteen to thirty-eight. Without exception, each one called me "Mom". I was always bewildered why my patients would address me thusly. When I affiliated at Akron Childrens' Hospital as a student, all my wee charges called me "Mom". They would stand at the end of their cribs waiting for me to make my rounds in the ward, and upon seeing me, they would jump up and down shouting, "Here comes our Mommy!" And, now I was everyone's mom again. I didn't have an ample bosom, or a generous figure or a motherly face. But I did care for them. Maybe they sensed that in me.

Every evening, the ambulatory patients would ask, "Mom, can I have a pass into town?" I would try to be stern as I cautioned them to be back in the ward by 2130 (9:30 P.M.). One burly pair, fifteen years my senior, asked "Mom" for passes too. If anyone missed curfew, it would have been this pair, but they never let me down and always returned with a gift for "Mom".

Mary Kay and I had never been close. Although the exigencies of the service had thrown us together since overseas training at Camp Beale, we were an unlikely pair. Mary Kay was volatile, outspoken, rough and often smutty. Her abrasive characteristics collided with my reserved, formal upbringing. (Mother was in her seventies before she said "darn" and the utterance completely startled her.) In a strange way, I found Mary Kay fascinating. During our time in the eighth floor surgery at the 334th, Mary Kay began presenting some puzzling behavior.

She began eating raw potatoes that she obtained from the kitchen. If we were not busy, she could be found sitting on the floor, with legs outstretched, leaning her back against a work table in the surgical supply room. She kept a stash of raw potatoes on a small table in our quarters. Bedtimes were difficult because Mary Kay would roll into our room nightly about midnight, highly inebriated. She always lit a cigarette, flopped on her bed, and that's as far as she got before she passed out. I dared not fall asleep until I could rescue the lighted cigarette, carefully removing it from between her fingers so as not to rouse her and incur her alcohol-driven anger. When I tried to talk to her in the morning, she would become belligerent and deny any memory of the incident.

One day, I found her in an awful temper. It seems that she had had a boyfriend whom she had left behind in Leyte. He had written to her offering to marry her by proxy. She was furious. Her cursing and recriminating against the absent boyfriend reverberated around the upstairs of the embassy. After that episode, she complained about getting fat and borrowed a skirt from one of the bigger girls.

I had always prided myself on my powers of observation. I could catch the most subtle nuances in my patients' conditions, but I had misfired totally on Mary Kay. All the clues were there; the food craving, the labile emotions, the fatigue, the weight gain, the absent boyfriend belatedly trying to do the right thing by proxy. Mary Kay was pregnant.

I did not know the army's policy on pregnancy. I had heard that the pregnant girls were sent to an army hospital stateside. Perhaps, fifty years ago, the thinking was that if we don't talk about it, it will go away. Not so, then, and not so, today. The problem has to be dealt with.

In Mary Kay's case, she would deal with it in her own way. She told no one except her current boyfriend. He was protective of her. He was loyal to her, and he married her. I learned much later that she had her baby, unassisted, in their living quarters. Her husband had married her to legitimize the child. There are too many unanswered questions to this story, and like so many of the loose ends that were left dangling whenever orders came to move on, I will never have a neat package with all the knots tied.

I was very happy to see Don. I may have known him a few short weeks in Leyte, but finding him again was like a reunion with a loved one from home. Don had been assigned to Special Services, a unit responsible for intra-service basketball, baseball and volleyball leagues and special events for service men. On our off duty time, we explored the surrounding countryside. We went hiking in the snow and had snowball fights on the slopes of Mt. "Fuji", climbed the bluffs around Yokohama, scouted the mansions on "Embassy Row" trying to get glimpses through the gates, and crawled around inside the head of the Great Buddha of Kamakura.

Kamakura is about eleven miles south of Yokohama. From about 1190 AD to 1590 AD, it was the political center of Japan. Many of the shoguns resided there and battled among themselves for supremacy and power. It lost its political importance when Tokyo became the capital of Japan. Its beauty and antiquity and the Great Buddha make it a favorite of tourists.

Daibutsu is the name given in Japan to the large statues of Buddha. The largest, in Nara on Honshu, is fifty-three feet high and dates from the eighth century. The Buddha of Kamakura is a bronze Daibutsu over forty-nine and a half feet high with four foot wide eyes made of gold. At the time of our visit, there were no restrictions keeping sightseers from inspecting the statue inside and out.

Through with our frolic, we were walking down the broad mall leading away from the statue when we were approached by a Japanese man. I dislike stereotyping, but he was everyone's idea of the Japanese persona. He was skinny with thinning black hair, thick glasses and large, slightly protruding teeth. He leaned slightly forward in a posture of obeisance, and his hands were folded in front of him and tucked into the sleeves of his kimomo. The Japanese never seemed to walk with long, purposeful strides but rather minced along with small steps, projecting a subservient image. In this manner, he hesitantly neared us, bowing and grinning broadly, and began words to this effect, "Would esteemed Americans honor me with their presence for tea in my home? I wish to practice my English with Americans." Actually, his English was more than adequate and practicing the language was a ploy to get us to accept his invitation. I was excited and more than willing to accompany him.

We entered a nicely kept little home. The back wall of the room was fashioned like a floor-to-ceiling display case with the display cubicles constructed in varying sizes to accomodate different pieces of art. The room, though typically sparse, was tastefully decorated with silk screens, little stands holding artful flower arrangements and art objects. I was most interested in an object on the low, square table in the middle of the room. It was an English translation of the Bible. I said, "Oh! I see you have a Bible. Are you Christian?" to which he replied, with much bowing and smiling, "Ah, yes, Christian and Buddha." He was taking no chances. He could either enter Heaven or Nirvana, whichever one took him first.

As our visit progressed, it became apparent what he was angling for. He was hungry and wanted any foodstuffs we might have. How pitiful that this obviously educated man, whose home reflected his good taste and standing in the community, felt called upon to bow and scrape to the Americans for food. Unknown to me, Don was in the habit of carrying rations in the jeep for just such an emergency. He brought an arm load of K-rations to our host. His eyes lit up and he was profuse in his gratitude. What he did next both moved me and delighted me. He hurried over to his display wall and took from a prominent place a tall, beautiful, ceremonial doll and brought her to me. She was twenty-four inches high, dressed in silk in her native costume, with her dark hair fashioned in the manner of the geisha. I had learned to accept a proffered gift. I had also learned that it is more difficult to be a gracious recipient than it is to be a magnanimous giver. I felt sad that he would relinquish a ceremonial doll that had probably been in his family for years.

I have had "Mioko", as I so named her, in my home for fifty-two years now. In every home in which we have lived, my husband has built a glass-enclosed niche in a wall to house her. He calls her his "Babe" and is almost as proud of her as I am. She won a ribbon for me at a doll show. I feel the Japanese gentleman who entrusted her to me would be pleased.

It was rewarding to me to have meaningful work to do. I had been disenchanted with my wastrel days at the monastery. However, my work schedule made deep rifts in my exploring time. I had become conditioned to view every circumstance as a learning opportunity. Understanding the Japanese people was particularly edifying for me.

They were painfully polite to foreigners and to each other. Their greetings were ritualistic, but as they wrapped themselves in a veneer of civility, they subverted their less tolerable impulses. It would be well for all of us to recognize that good manners are an act of kindness to our fellow wayfarers.

Despite the deprivations of a war economy, they had a capacity for joy, of sheer delight in the most simple things, such as the mamma-sans' pleasure in this Occidental girl's lipstick and nail polish. They did everything with a light touch. Their laughter tinkled; their running steps were nimble and small; their movements graceful. I can understand how we appeared ungainly and boorish with our loud voices, raucous laughter and heavy tread.

Their benign demeanor belied a firm resolve, an enduring patience, a meticulous attention to detail, and a fanatic loyalty to their homeland. None of this is bad, but it was this national character that made them such a formidable enemy. I understand that, in my capacity as a healer, I viewed them from a different aspect than our fighting men who were forced to confront them on the battlefield. My contacts with the people - not the soldier or the politician - always resulted in a positive experience.

Our off-duty times did not always coincide, but when they did, Don and I would visit little villages, shrines in out of the way places, Tokyo's Imperial Hotel and Fuji-View Hotel.

In one small village were many little tots, swathed in heavy padded kimonos, taking their exercise in the pale winter sunshine. There is nothing more adorable than the young of any genre, and none any cuter than little Japanese children. Their curiosity about us overcame their shyness, and we soon had attracted a gathering. It was cold, and they all had runny noses. I had a box of tissues, and I went through the group dispensing tissues to each. Little hands reached out for the "gift" from the American lady. To my dismay, they began tucking the tissues into their kimono sleeves. I demonstrated with a tissue on my own nose, but no, they were going to save them in their kimono sleeves. So, I proceeded to pass out extra tissues, one to save and one to use. That didn't work either, for the extras went up the kimono sleeves too.

I have diligently searched the maps for a little town called Enoshima. Many of the Japanese towns end in "shima". Perhaps the town of my search is too small to warrant space on the maps. Its only access was by causeway at low tide. The village was so tiny that, upon reaching its narrow shore, it rose abruptly, the houses clinging to the precipitous sides of the tall cliff. After gaining its summit, it dipped treacherously down the back side that faced the sea. No dwellings perched on the windward side of the cliff.

Don and I had practiced on the bluffs around Yokohama and felt confident enough to descend to the rocks below. It was a tortuous climb. The waves crashed against the rocks sending spray shooting high and drenching us as it fell back into the sea. We had a fragile toe-hold on the slippery rocks and sought a less precarious footing by continuing our climb at an oblique angle across the face of the cliff. We had clambered over some huge boulders slipping and sliding to the other side. There we discovered a crevice in the tumble of rocks. Closer inspection revealed a cave. The opening was small, but once through it, one descended a sharp, narrow incline that opened into a large underground amphitheater. The opening was above high tide, but once inside, the cave was below sea level.

In the dim light that filtered through the opening, we recognized that we were in a shrine. All the appurtenances of one of the Japanese places of worship were there. There was a mystical aura about the shrine. We found ourselves speaking in hushed tones. Every sound we made had a hollow ring as if to alert their gods.The crashing of the sea outside sounded like a distant roar. I felt like an intruder. I didn't belong there. Is it possible that not even all the townspeople knew of its existence? And who had made the dangerous climb down into this very hidden, secret place and strung the little white pieces of paper that were a supplication to their deities? Or was it a shrine for seafarers who made their way to the rocks from the sea?

We made our way up the cliff, traversed the ridge to the other end of the little rock strewn mountain, hiked down the town side and hugged the narrow spit of land below the town to where we had left the jeep. The townspeople paid no attention to us at all. They did not exhibit the usual curiosity about Americans that we had come to expect.

Some of my recollections are very precious, and the discovery of the " Secret Shrine " is one of them.

American architect, Frank Lloyd Wright, designed the Imperial Hotel in Tokyo. It was constructed on a floating foundation so that during an earthquake, it could move and sway with the convulsing earth. The fires that ignited as the result of a major earthquake in 1923 burned Yokohama to the ground and destroyed sixty-five per cent of Tokyo, but the Imperial Hotel withstood the quake and the ensuing fires.

It was to the Imperial Hotel that a group of us had gone to sample Tokyo's burgeoning night life. We were in the sixth month of the occupation of Japan and Tokyo was already exhibiting all the trappings of a prewar cosmopolitan city. The hotel was a fascinating landmark. I am grateful that I had a chance to see this architectual marvel that had escaped earthquakes and war and fire before it fell victim to the wrecking ball to make way for some new development.

The FujiView Hotel was a resort that boasted of Mt. Fujiyama as its sentinel. It was being used as an R and R (rest and recreation) facility for the American forces. If one had been overseas long enough and got tired enough, one became eligible for R and R. We at the 334th were being scheduled for two glorious weeks there.

Don and I planned a preview look at Fuji-View. It was approximately fifty miles south-west of Yokohama. He had an enlisted man driver, but on this occasion, I was driving. The roads were very narrow, no more than a ribbon bisecting the rice paddies. There was no curbing, no berm, more like a levee between fields. I was doing fine until I moved to the left to accomodate an approaching vehicle, whereupon I slid off the road and tipped us over in a rice paddy. (Japan drives on the left side as does England.) Three farmers, who were spring planting, hurried over with a sizeable tree trunk, and using it as a fulcrum, righted the jeep and pushed it back on the road. My pride was hurt more than I was. We were all a little damp from the rice paddy but otherwise, unscathed.

Officers were assigned drivers from the motor pool. I had met Don's driver on other occasions when he had chauffeured us on outings. He was a beautiful young boy with the kind of pink and white flawless complexion that would be the envy of any girl. He looked as if he had yet to shave. He was easy-going and congenial and pleasant to have around.

One day, he asked to speak to me privately. It seems that he had contracted gonorrhea for the fourth time and was afraid to show up at sick call again for the same reason as the previous three times. He had his plan all worked out and needed only my acquiescence. I was to meet him at some prearranged rendezvous and give him the requisite penicillin shots.

Completely devoid of guile, he proceeded to tell me about his conquests of Japanese maids. He said the mamma-sans liked him and wanted him for their daughters, "But", he continued, "I never kiss 'em. Their breath's bad so I never kiss 'em." He had no conception of cause and effect or consequences. He wouldn't "kiss 'em", but he would get gonorrhea from them.

Of course, I refused his request and explained that it was crucial that he go to sick call again. I lectured him about the hazards of abusing his body and cautioned him that the disease would become antibiotic resistant if he continued to pursue his present behavior. (With talk today about antibiotic resistant bacteria, it may surprise today's readers that, fifty years ago, we were aware of organisms becoming resistant.)

All soldiers had seen the training films, attended the lectures and had been instructed about

venereal disease. I felt sad that this personable young
man was jeopardizing his future by his irresponsible
behavior.

Here, I mention my urgency for a rest room to point out
that the people outside the cities were still very much afraid of
us. We were in the hinterlands, and people and dwellings were
scarce. At length, we came upon a little house. A young women
was standing on a small porch holding a baby. When we
stopped, she clutched the baby to her and seemed to shrink in
terror. The men made no move to approach her leaving me to
near her and ask, " Benjo a dok adesta? " (I cannot vouch for
the spelling.) That phrase is the first I learned, one of
considerable importance to me. The woman relaxed a little,
probably because she did not feel as threatened by one of her
sex.

She indicated that I come inside, but first I had to
unbuckle and unlace my combat boots and remove them.
(When one is in a hurry, that requirement was a maddening
delay.) Once inside, I was shown to the typical tiny closet,
maybe thirty inches square, with a hole in the floor that was
open to the ground below. The men went around to the back of
the house and emulated the natives.

Fuji-View Hotel was everything I dreamed it would be;
beautiful, luxurious, exciting with interior pools all over, some
connected to suites for the private use of the residents. There
were gardens enclosed in ones' own courtyard and larger
gardens where one could walk or just sit and meditate.

We hiked in the snow, watched some Japanese boys
ice-skating on a pond, made an acquaintance with a small
blond German girl, and had dinner in a well-appointed dining
room.

From our table, I could look through a door that opened
into a large private dining room. I could see a large group of
elegant men and women dressed for dinner in tuxedos and long
dinner gowns. They comprised a group of European aristocrats
who had been stranded in Japan at the outbreak of the war. I
do not know their national allegiances, but they were detained
in Japan, and they waited out the war in the plush
surroundings of Fuji-View.

I was eagerly anticipating R and R in and around the environs of the resort and Mt. "Fuji".

Alas, in my dreams - only in my dreams.

I had become aware of a vague uneasiness nagging me. I was losing my home and family. Oh, I always held them close in my heart and mind, but I was losing the perception of their reality. That reality was dependent upon the concrete evidence of their existence by letters and boxes from home, things I could touch and smell that had been handled by them.

Through some fault in the system, it had been weeks since I had received any mail, and regarding boxes, I received one during my overseas tour. I knew that my family and their friends had all sent goodies and trinkets. I hope someone enjoyed them. The lone box that had made its way to me contained hair ribbons and a home permanent. I had meant to get the Chief Nurse off my back by doing something with my hair.

It was rumored that there was a bottleneck on the west coast holding up the mail. With the absence of mail, I lost the life line that kept us connected. I found my family slipping farther and farther away from the flesh and blood of my life in Japan. I pictured my home as in a fairy tale, peopled with a fairy tale family.

I am ashamed to say that I stopped writing to Mother and Father. It was as if all I had left was their memory that I carried with me. I learned later how cruel was my act of omission.

It was a strange phenomenon. I had been overseas only seven months. What must the soldiers who had been gone two, three and four years have felt? Was it this same mental climate that had caused Joel to imagine life with me more real than with his wife at home? And was it because our life was in the here and now in Japan that it gained the status of permanency? With permanency, we seek structure and stability. We deluded ourselves into believing that this fleeting interlude was the reality.

It was in these circumstances that Don and I sought to build our future in this foreign land. Why not? Home was but a figment. To further our plans, Don started at the beginning. He bought me a ring. He told me to keep it, and after thoughtful prayer, if I was in accord with all the implications accepting a ring entailed, I should wear it on my finger when next we met. That would be my answer.

I put the ring on my finger.

Taking a break from surgery on the roof of the 334th "department store" hospital.

*One burly pair asked "Mom" for passes too. If anyone
missed curfew, it would have been this pair, but they never
let me down and always returned with a gift for "Mom".*

The great Buddha (Daibutsu) of Kamakura.

Meredith in Tokyo which was already exhibiting the trappings of a prewar cosmopolitan city.

a

b

c

d

At the base of Mt. "Fuji":
a) Making an acquaintance with a small, blue-
   eyed German girl.
b) A snowball fight with Don.
c) Watching Japanese boys ice skating on a pond.
d) Snow fields.

The Old Schoolhouse

Although we were still attached to the 334th, some of us were sent to an abandoned schoolhouse that had been converted into a hospital. The classrooms were the wards. I thought that we had been sent there to clean the place up. I had never seen a facility currently in service that was as filthy. Even in field hospitals, in primitive, dangerous situations, hygienic and sanitary measures are put into practice. That's what a hospital is; to perform surgery and treat battlefield wounds as near to the front as possible in less than optimum circumstances, but employing sterile techniques and keeping the area free of contamination. The schoolhouse did not have to contend with the aforementioned conditions, and still, it could not come up to minimum principles of hygiene.

The schoolhouse was being run by corpsmen. They had done the best they could, but they were lacking in a standard of practice that was conducive to getting patients well.

The hospital was a two-story wooden building with classrooms on either side of a central corridor. I was appalled when I entered the first ward of my assignment. The room was dirty; the patients were dirty; their bandages were dirty; and the men were demoralized. There was no response from them when I entered, just sullen, tired stares. They ate their meals with tongue blades. Even the soldier's mess gear contained utensils, a knife, fork and spoon.

My work was cut out for me. I wanted to start every place at once. Like a Dutch hausfrau, I scrubbed the room, my patients, everything in sight. I started investigating what was under the dirty bandages, cleaning and debrising incisions, sores, as I went. Getting eating utensils was a matter of requisitioning for them.

The teacher's dais at one end of the room gave space to the bed of a very sick man. I determined that he would not begin to improve until I inserted a tube through his nose into his stomach using Wangensteen's suction apparatus to siphon off putrifying stomach contents.

Wangensteen's method was a techique for relieving postoperative distention, nausea, and vomiting and certain instances of mechanical bowel obstruction. It involves hooking together a series of stoppered bottles in such a manner as to create vacuum and suction. The old Wangensteen would look primitive next to today's sophisticated machines that automatically suction and regulate. Even the nomenclature is different for the new apparatus.

My objective was to obtain a Wangensteen. My problem was that there wasn't such a thing. I learned that miscellaneous, broken and damaged equipment had been tossed into trash barrels in back of the schoolhouse, so that's where I went, to the dump. I rummaged through the trash hoping to find something I could use. It was a treasure trove of all kinds of bottles, snippets of rubber tubing and small, broken sections of glass tubing. I boiled up my conglomeration of pieces; strung them together, glass to rubber to glass and so on until I had the lengths I needed; hooked them into the bottles in such a way as to create a suction; attached one end to my patient's stomach tube, and voila, I had a Wangensteen. It looked like something out of a modern sculptor's nightmare, but it worked. And, more importantly, my patient began to improve.

The adage, "Cleanliness is next to Godliness" accurately described my ward. The improvement in my patients was both rapid and dramatic. Their morale and their self-esteem rose in proportion to the respect shown to them and the care given to them. I told myself, "Aha! It's the woman's touch!" In part, that may be true, but I think the anxiety of languishing in those slovenly surroundings, and feeling trapped and powerless to pull themselves out of it in their weakened condition retarded their recovery.

It was acutely obvious to the corpsmen what we had been doing in our respective wards, and they resented our actions even if it meant improvement for the patients. They were heard to say many times, "We were doing okay until you women came here. Who needs you anyway?" I had never before encountered the hostility toward me and the other nurses that was in evidence at the schoolhouse. It got so bad that I actually had to "pull rank" on a corpsman, the first and only time I had done so. Pulling rank is when a superior officer gives a direct order with an implied threat that disobedience to that order would result in disciplinary action.

A small office was being utilized as a central supply where one could get needed equipment. I had gone there to order smaller gauge needles for my intra-muscular syringes. The needles in use at the time of my takeover were what can best be described as "horse" needles, those large, bruising needles that further exacerbated tissue trauma at injection sites. I encountered a big, surly, disrespectful, "make me" bully in charge of the supplies. In answer to my request, he leaned far over the counter with a menacing, in-your-face sneer and impudently said, "No! You can't have them. We have been using the large needles since before you came, and that's all you're gonna get!" Oh my! He was asking for it. I was small, but in my "Great Katrinka" guise, I was mighty, and he shouldn't have messed with Katrinka. I pulled rank ......and I got my needles.

My next ward was on the second floor of the schoolhouse. I encountered much the same conditions as with the first ward but with an additional duty. I was to transform a former infantry man into a corpsman. This new circumstance grew out of the need to retrain the many combat soldiers for non-combat duties so that they could fulfill functions in the Occupation Army. That is how I met Walt, a big, tall, husky infantry man.

All went well until I sliced the top of one of my fingers as I was cleaning the area around a particularly large, revolting carbuncle on the back of a soldier's neck. The razor blade that cut me was grossly contaminated with purulent exudate. I ran to the dressing cart that was in the hallway yelling for my infantryman-turned-corpsman to help me. I was holding my finger over a basin. It was bleeding profusely, and I encouraged it further by milking it. A generalized septicemia could result from the introduction of bacteria through a much smaller wound than this, and I wanted the blood to wash the contaminants away. Meanwhile, I instructed my corpsman to pour volumes of alcohol directly into the wound. Then I told him how to bandage the finger. I thought he had done quite well. I did not learn until shortly after the incident how shook up he was from the blood and from his initiation in dressing a wound, minor though it was.

The medical officer of the ward was my immediate superior. He came to me and said, "Hey! What did you do to that boy? He has asked for a transfer. He told me, 'That nurse scares me to death!'." I was devastated. I thought that I had been so good to him. Besides, how did I know that a big six-foot four-inch guy would be afraid of me, and I hadn't even put on my "Great Katrinka" cloak?

He came to visit me often. He gave me a photograph with the sentiment on the back that read, "To a nurse a fellow is proud to work with. Love, Walt.", but he never worked with me again.

I can still rub my thumbnail over a ridge of scar tissue on the finger I cut and remember how it came to be there.

At the school house, we were working twelve hours a day, seven days a week. I had much more to learn about the country, but my outings were postponed until such time when I could wrangle a half day off, this usually once a month.

When my shift on my ward was finished, I would often stop by the surgery to see if Mary Kay needed any help. She had set up a surgery in one of the dingy classrooms. With its naked lights bulbs swinging from a wire and lone operating table, it was a far cry from the surgery at the department store. Nonetheless, emergencies did come in at odd times, and it was at those times that I would stay over and be her assistant. Such incidents extended our day to fifteen hours or more.

Upon returning to the embassy, we would head for the kitchen where Mamma-san would be waiting to rustle up an after hours meal. Depending upon its availability, she would save special treats for us, like a steak.

Even at this time, I had not caught on that Mary Kay was pregnant. She was very tired, but then we all were, and her fatigue did not strike me as unusual. I was caught up in a vortex of activity that extended to my off duty time because I did not want to lose a minute of time with Don or give up any chances for exploring and learning. So it was a shock to me to discover that I had lost one full size in clothing when I sought to obtain an additional pair of O.D. (olive drab) slacks. When one is running on some hidden reserve, one does not stop to check the gauges to ascertain the fuel level, and I wasn't out of fuel yet!

In connection with Don's job in Special Services, he had formed a basketball league. So that we could be together during basketball season, he taught me how to keep score, and I became the official score keeper of the league. I have a certificate that says;

ARMY ATHLETICS in JAPAN

United States Occupational Forces

This is to certify that

Lt. Meredith Miller

was a participant in

BASKETBALL-MASCOT

Robt. L Eichelberger
Commanding General, 8th Army

I had learned a new skill and took my duties seriously. Although I always had a monitor at my side as a checker when I kept score, that fact did not help me during a hotly contested game one night.

Mary Kay's boyfriend was on one of the teams. I had called him out on four fouls, and I found myself on the receiving end of the wrath and vengeance of both of them. Mary Kay accused me of favoritism, cheating and all sorts of devious things that hadn't occurred to me. I became her avowed enemy, and she never spoke to me again. Mary Kay was not my favorite, but I was sorry she had added the weight of spite and choler on her already stressful situation.

Don played a wicked game of ping-pong. He and I were at the officers' club having a hard-slamming game. I wasn't too shabby myself and wanted to show him I wasn't a pushover. Among the spectators was a colonel who introduced himself. In the ensuing conversation, he said he had a surprise (these colonels and their surprises!) if I would meet him at a certain place the following night. I was game. The following evening, Don picked me up when I got off duty, and we hurried over to the "place". I hadn't had time to change from my seersucker wrap-around to my proper uniform. We had been instructed to go to the second floor of the building to which we had been directed.

There I entered a classroom already in session, and at the head of the class was the colonel. He was teaching a college level psychology class. The army had instituted a program whereby students, whose college had been interrupted or who had missed their college entrance date because of the call to duty, could pick up credits that would be transferable to any college in the United States. I was ecstatic about having this chance, and I was flattered that the colonel had invited me to participate.

My pride soon turned to embarrassment. I had meant to impress him with my sincerity and my "intellectual depth". I had meant to make a good showing in this classroom of men. Alas, my twelve hour days had caught up with me. Every night I fell asleep in class as soon as I sat down and my body acknowledged that it was tired. I could play an active game of ping-pong, but I didn't dare sit down and break the momentum of the frenetic pace I had demanded of myself.

As fate would have it, I would not have been able to complete the semester. Without warning, I, along with most of the girls who had been together during our tour of duty in Japan, got my orders to be rotated to the States. I was due for my turn at R and R and Fuji-View two weeks hence. Someone else would enjoy my time slot there.

Mary Kay would not be with us. She had married Hal and would stay in Japan with him. I do not know what strings they pulled to keep this arrangement given the complicated procedure couples were required to follow before permission was granted to marry. I suspected that the red tape was designed to discourage couples from taking a hasty route to possible regret.

I geared up for the final push.....home.

He gave me a photograph with the sentiment, "To a nurse a fellow is proud to work with. Love, Walt." but he never worked with me again.

HOMEWARD

Every man and woman in the service dreams of home. I dreamed of home too, but I had already lost the reality of my home and was unable to actually visualize my going there. Many were those who spent their stint in the service in a vacuum with nothing to sustain them except their fantasies of home. They existed in limbo, stunning their senses with alcohol, sexual gratification or any other creature comfort they could find. The fighting men had a whole different set of circumstances that assaulted their senses from danger, terror, physical deprivations, and pain and exhaustion. They functioned on a more primitive level of survival of kill or be killed. It was nearly impossible to retain any semblance of civilization. At the odd times when they were not numb with fatigue, they too fell back on dreams of home to renew themselves.

The armed services were aware of the psychological pitfalls lurking to waylay the susceptible. Their attempts at normalizing the military environment could be found in athletic leagues, entertainment, books, and clubs, but those things were not the first priority of the armed forces. One had to recognize that the military was not your conventional environment and try to go forward from there.

I could not live in limbo. I had to make sense of my situation. I had to establish something meaningful, to become involved with my surroundings, and in so doing, I did not dwell on self. I was not nearly so concerned with what was happening to me as with what I could be doing.

The army was frustrating in that respect. Plucked from one situation and transplanted to another, being manipulated like a pawn in a chess game, negated any opportunity for completion or a sense of accomplishment. I never knew the final resolution of a case or the fate of the many friends I made.

So it was with mixed emotions that I learned I was going home. I wasn't ready. I hadn't finished my work here. By what rationale had the army decided to sweep us all off the roster when we finally had a well-run organization and were in a position to accomplish much?

Perhaps I wasn't adaptable enough. I always threw myself into the work at hand and then, was loathe to leave, willy-nilly, for another situation. My work was here, not at home.

In my secret heart, I knew some of the foregoing was a smoke screen to blot out the need to address the decision making that my going home would activate. As long as I was in the service, I did not have to contemplate any future beyond the present. I was not alone in thinking we would be in the army forever, in Japan forever.

There was a reluctance by some to confront the prospect of separation from the service. We described them as those who had "found a home in the army". No matter how odious or dangerous their job, they did not have to concern themselves with food, clothing and shelter. They made good soldiers, but faced with the prospect of fending for themselves in civilian life, they often failed. We called them "maladjusted civilians". Had I "found a home in the army"? I liked having the basics provided for me, leaving my mind free to perform my duty. However, I was determined that I was not going to be a "maladjusted civilian".

Such was my state of mind as I prepared to vacate the 334th Station Hospital for the Replacement Depot, nicknamed by all the "Repple Depple". This final stop in Japan was a way station for personnel awaiting transportation home.

Our commanding officer had a ritual I had not experienced at other stations. Common practice was to get our orders, grab our gear and run when the transportation arrived. This colonel sat behind his desk in his office and gave audience to each of us, individually, behind closed doors. We were required to be impeccable in Class "A's", to enter at his command, salute, listen to his words of wisdom, salute and be dismissed. We were given an opportunity to speak if we had anything important to say. I had planned a speech that would emphasize the positive benefits of my tenure in service, but when I stood before this rigid, intimidating man, my speech took flight and I could only gulp a, "Thank you, sir," to his, "Goodbye and good luck.", and that was the final excision of my army career.

At the "Repple Depple" was all manner of red tape to be satisfied before we were free to go. We filled out customs declarations. All hand and hold luggage had to be inspected. Once inspected, our luggage that would go into the hold of the ship was no longer available to us. I had nothing to declare because I had sent all my goodies home. One of my patients had made me a foot locker size wooden crate. Then he helped me pack my samurai sword, my Japanese fisherman, my ceremonial doll and several other treasures, nailed the lid down, shipped it out, and all that was left, was to pray. With the incidences of theft, I was exceedingly fortunate that my memorabilia made it home.

I had sent my helmet home with a merchant seaman who sailed on the Liberty ship, Helena Modjeska. He had promised to mail it to my parents' home. Instead, he kept a nice souvenir for himself.

> The Liberty ships of World War II were built by Kaiser Shipbuilding. In the interest of expediency, they were welded instead of riveted. This practice weakened the integrity of the construction, making them prone to breaking in half. The Helena Modjeska subsequently broke in two in the English Channel. Mayhap my helmet is at the bottom of the English Channel?

Then we had to be inspected by a physician. I have a certificate that says I was found to be free of vermin.

After three days at the "Repple Depple", we were eligible for a daily pass from 0800 to 2245 (10:45 P.M.), and also after three days, whom should I see coming into the barracks? Clenie! There were organizational changes in many of the units, and Clenie's was one of them. I had not seen her since we were dispersed on tdy assignments at the monastery in Luzon. She had been stationed with a marine unit in Sasebo and Fukuoka on the island of Kyushu.

I had planned an illegal flight with one of the air force men who flew an A-20 and who had business in Kyushu. He would see that I got to Clenie's base. Bad weather cancelled the

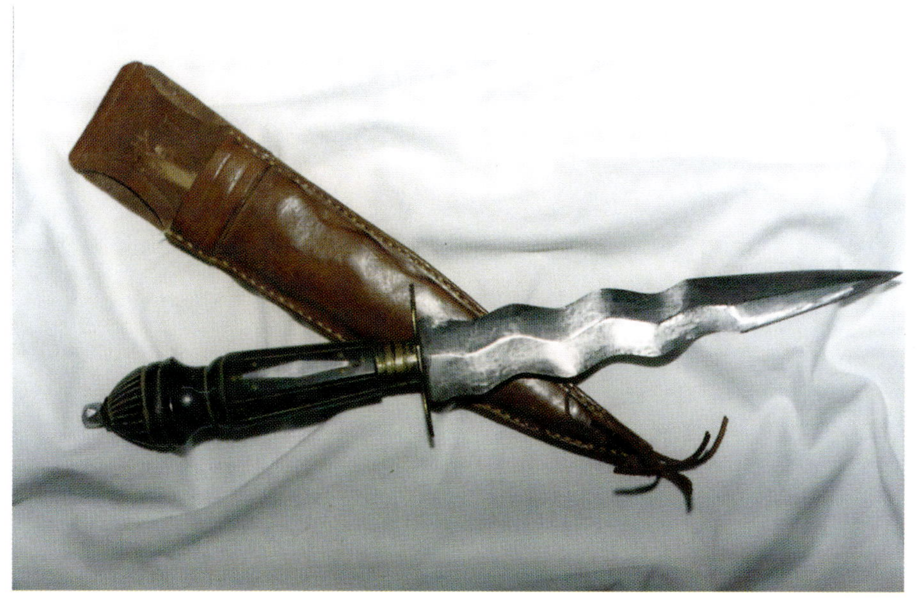

I believed I could fend off an enemy assault with my Philippine dagger...as long as there were not too many of them.

Japanese water color depicts me in Joel's flight jacket with his scarf wound around my head like a turban.

*From a prominent place in the wall, he took a beautiful
ceremonial doll and brought her to me.*

Certificate from "The Domain of the Golden Dragon."

flight, and no doubt, that fact spared me from getting into trouble again. We had to satisfy ourselves with buzzing the Japanese fishermen in the harbor - also a frowned upon activity.

Concurrent with my move to the "Repple Depple", was Don's transfer some distance from Yokohama. Don and I were happy together. We blissfully took our life in Japan for granted, unconcerned about all our tomorrows. We were sharing a common environment unencumbered by any baggage from our respective backgrounds. What would happen to us at home when we had to confront such considerations as ethnology and religion? Those things mattered not one whit when we were together in Japan away from family conditioning and expectations.

We saw each other as much as we could within the confines of his schedule and my daily passes. There was a poignancy to those last hours that we clung to each other. Goodbyes had never been easy for me even among friends. With someone for whom I cared deeply, it was like an amputation. I would experience one of life's deepest heart-aches, separation, and I could not help thinking about all the women who had seen their men off to war, and who had suffered their absence for many years.

I was at the "Repple Depple" for fifteen days, and on April 9, 1946, along with several nurses, a troop of U.S.O. girls (A service organization dedicated to entertaining the troops.) and several hundred G.I.'s, I left Japan on the U.S.S. Marine Serpent. Our passage was completed in twelve days as opposed to the twenty-nine day voyage on the Marigold. The Serpent was larger, newer, faster and our route from Honshu to Seattle was less than the distance from San Pedro, California to Manila.

The Marine Serpent was contracted with the Kaiser Company of Vancouver, Washington by the Maritime Commission. Her keel was laid in November of 1944, and she was launched in June of 1945.

Following the cessation of hostilities, she took part in the massive sealift carrying occupation troops to the Far East and bringing veterans from the Pacific Theater home to the United States.

Between the end of October 1945 to the end of February 1946, she completed two runs from San Francisco to the Philippines. Between March to June of 1946, the Serpent made two runs to Japan and back sealifting troops. (From this history, I have learned that ours was the Serpent's third voyage being sealifted from Japan to Seattle in April of 1946.)

She remained in the Maritime Commission Reserve Fleet for five years until she was called into service during the Korean Conflict. She made six voyages out of west coast ports to Japan and South Korea. During this time, some of her duties included transporting North Korean POW's among the Korean offshore islands.

After an uneasy peace, she made seven voyages to the Far East carrying replacement troops and returning to the United States with veterans of the Korean Conflict.

Following a brief period of reduced operational status, in December of 1954, she was pressed into service again for the Vietnam conflict. For the next four months, she sailed along the Indochina coast transporting Vietnamese refugees from the Communist north to South Vietnam. She also evacuated French troops and supplies southward to Saigon and Tourane.

Her duties completed in troubled Southeast Asia, the Serpent was placed on reduced status in August of 1955. She was struck from the Navy roster and remained berthed in Puget Sound, in Olympia Washington through 1969. I have no history of the U.S.S. Marine Serpent beyond this date. Perhaps this ship, which earned three battle stars for her service in Korea, has joined the other brave ladies of the sea on the scrap heap.

I had left a note on Clenie's cot telling her I would see her in the states. She followed on another ship three days later, and in such a manner, we zig-zagged through the military separation procedure.

Don came down to the dock the night before we left the harbor, one lonely figure staring up at me. From the deck railing high above, I reached for him with arms outstretched straining to shrink the tantalizing distance between us.

The northern route across the Pacific was rougher than the first trip. Some of the girls never left their bunks the whole voyage. We were segregated from the soldiers who staked out space on the main deck to take the air and sun.

There was an incident that sullied all of us and dropped a pall over what was otherwise a pleasant voyage. The army officer in charge of us ordered all the female personnel into the salon one day. As we wended our way through the hundreds of soldiers on the deck - some of whom pulled my pigtails that were tied with the ribbons Mother had sent - we had no idea the reason for our summons.

It had come to the officer's attention that one of the nurses was prostituting herself every night after hours. She would go out on the deck and sell her services for forty dollars a "client". He knew who the wretched girl was but preferred to accuse all of us. We squirmed in discomfort and embarrassment as he harangued. The U.S.O. girls, who did not come under the same auspices as the rest of us, were heard to say, "We don't have to sit here and listen to this.", whereupon they walked out. But we were held captive as he painted us all with the same brush. At that odd moment in time, my mind turned homeward and to my parents, and how they would not have condoned my being subjected to this man's denunciations, and how they would have come to my defense. In such a manner, I tuned out the vile names he reserved for all of us and, mentally, dwelled on home.

One person tarnished us all. It wasn't the first time I had heard stories of prostitution. I had heard that some girls went home rich. Thankfully, I did not know their identities.

When we crossed the International Date Line on April 16, 1946, we gained back the day we had lost on our first crossing. A certificate from "The Domain of the Golden Dragon, Ruler of the 180th Meridian" goes on to say that "Meredith J. Miller, having been found sane and worthy to be numbered a dweller of the FAR EAST, has been gathered into my fold and duly initiated into the SILENT MYSTERIES of the FAR EAST etc." and signed by the GOLDEN DRAGON. We also had what we called a "Short-Snorter" which was a long string of paper currency from different countries all pasted together. The greater the number of countries, the longer the "Short-Snorter".

The music hits of the 1940's blared over the loudspeakers such as "It's Been a Long, Long Time" - I loved that one -, "Don't Sit Under the Apple Tree", "BoogieWoogie Bugle Boy", "I'll Be With You in Apple Blossom Time". Or remember "Green Eyes", "Tangerine ", "What'll I Do "? Then there was Irving Berlin's "The Girl That I Marry", a beautiful song that got the fellows all wistful and romantic. I took exception to it, especially the part about:

"A doll I can carry,
the girl that I marry"
or
"I'll be sittin'
next to her and
she'll purr like a kitten"

because I wasn't a doll, and I didn't want to be someone's kitten. I wanted to be a partner.

Joan Crawford's "Mildred Pierce" was showing on the motion picture screen in the salon.

I vacillated between lamenting my life and love that I had left behind in the Orient and my growing excitement of seeing my country, my family and home. I embraced the spiritual renewal of an awe-inspiring Easter sunrise service on the deck of the ship with the vast ocean meeting the sky as our cathedral. A pale sun burned through the mist and chill of the early morning air as we stood on the damp deck with a gentle sea spray falling on us. It was April 21, 1946. It had been a year ago that a small group of travelers had wended its way up a hill to Easter services at Martinsburg, West Virginia.

Later that day, it was time to stand at the deck rail and strain our eyes for the first small grey line on the horizon. The ship would steam through Puget Sound and dock at Seattle, Washington. Busses would transport us to Ft. Lawton. We would set foot on our native soil.

We hoisted our gear and waited in line on the deck to disembark. As we came down the gangplank, we saw the ubiquitous Red Cross ladies with their coffee and doughnuts, but, no! Wait! It was MILK and doughnuts! Milk! I knew I was really home.

The most conspicuous point to make about Ft. Lawton - at least to us returnees - involved the mess hall. We did not stand in a chow line but were served at large tables by Italian prisoners-of-war, a happy, comical, joyful bunch who obviously made the most of any situation. We were served country style with huge platters of steaks, large bowls of mashed potatoes, fresh vegetables, heaps of corn on the cob, stacks of fresh sliced tomatoes, fresh butter, home baked bread and jam and all the milk and ice cream we could eat. I think I recouped the clothing size I lost in Japan in one sitting at this gorgeous table groaning with food. The army did itself proud with this gesture of thanks to all its returning guys and gals.

A post-script to my intemperance at "wolfing down", in carefree overindulgence, my land's abundance was that my body reacted with a severe allergic reaction trying to assimilate all the "alien" foods I had ingested.

A train ride through the beautiful, majestic northwest of Montana, through North Dakota and Minnesota, brought us to Madison, Wisconsin where I give credence to the second half of my title, "and chased troop trains."

We had a layover in Madison. I was totally engrossed in a book as we waited in the station's waiting room for our next rail connection. At some point, I became aware that the room had grown strangely quiet. I looked up from my book and saw that they were gone, all gone! I held my hat, and with my purse dangling from its shoulder strap banging me on the hip, I rushed out of the station. The train had cleared the station, and I saw the back of the last car rolling down the tracks. Hiking my skirts to give my legs freedom to run, I roared after the train with the all too familiar, "Come on, Miller! Come on, Miller!" ringing in my ears. At the connection of the last two cars were arms outstretched ready to snare me, and they hauled me aboard - for the last time.

As a result of my frantic dash from the station, I had forgotten my book and musette bag. Encumbered with two extra articles, I would never have caught the train. A nameless lieutenant, whom I never met, went all the way back to Madison to retrieve them. I made up my mind that I would learn to be punctual even if it was my last conscious act on earth!

And, I have been punctual ever since...... fanatically so.

Ft. Sheridan, Illinois, the final stop, and then home. This was a separation center where we would undergo our final physical; pick up promotion papers and final leave orders; receive mustering out pay and information on retaining our G.I. life insurance; and participate in a compulsory, body measuring study to develop criteria for sizing womens' clothing.

All the red tape was satisfied, catalogued, stamped and filed, and like a revolving door, I was out, "separated". I was experiencing sensations similar to the released prisoner when the gates clang shut behind him.

After a long, convoluted journey that had begun at the 334th and ended here in Illinois, I suddenly wanted to get it over with and abruptly exchanged my train ticket for a flight to Cleveland's Hopkins Airport.

It was midnight when the plane set down in Cleveland. I shared a cab with another officer who had business in Akron. At 0200 - I mean at 2:00 A.M. I must get used to talking "Civilian" - I was in the driveway of my home in Akron, Ohio. I had carried my door key half way around the world, and now, I would bring it out and let myself into my house.

I crept up the stairs, like a thief in the night, and stealthily crawled into my waiting bed. There, my parents found me in the morning.

I was home.

Broken Ship Stuck In Channel

This unusual photo shows the American ship Helena Modjeska, broken in two and aground on the "Goodwin sands in the English channel, after a severe gale lashed the southern coast of England,--AP Wirephoto.

The Liberty ships were welded instead of riveted which weakened the integrity of the structure making them prone to breaking in half.

The U.S.S. Marine Serpent took me home.

EPILOGUE

Vintage Wine

Through the years, whenever the subject came up, my father could be heard muttering, "She never conformed. She never conformed."

Why couldn't I have conformed just this once? Why did I sneak home in the middle of the night? Why hadn't I called them and informed them of the arrival of my flight into Cleveland so that they could have participated in the kind of joyful reunion that television portrayed of the "Desert Storm"[22] returnees? I don't know. Selfish though it sounds now, I didn't want to talk about it. One would have thought that I suffered great trauma. I didn't. I admit to wanting time to sort out my thoughts and to decide the thrust and direction of my future. Mother and Father were perplexed, but they did not press me for an accounting. My young brother was overjoyed to see me and used the flimsiest opportunity to show me off. My sister, grateful for my safe return, viewed me somewhat with skepticism, wondering if I was somehow different.

Clenie's parents had moved from my immediate neighborhood to Aaronsburg, Pennsylvania in the Allegheny Mountains during her absence. Clenie's father was restoring a historical stagecoach inn. It was there that I met Clenie for our own private R and R, the one that we missed in Japan.

We spent idyllic days hiking the mountains, picking fresh vegetables from the garden for Clenie's mother to cook for supper, sleeping in ancient bedrooms with foot thick, stone walls. We listened to the mice, whose ancestors had been there long before us, scratching in the walls, and we carried on late night conversations from her room to mine. We got civilized only long enough to travel to Philadelphia and other larger towns to, halfheartedly, fill out job applications at the local hospitals.

The whole interlude tranquilized our souls. I never wanted it to end, but my dreamy days were interrupted by a call from my mother. Don would be calling from Japan a few days hence. I hurried home and waited. Don was coming home.

It was almost summer of 1946. I would see Don before he returned to college in the fall. Meanwhile, I took a position at old Peoples' Hospital, now Akron General Medical Center. There I served as night superintendent of the hospital while the permanent superintendent was on a leave of absence. This I enjoyed. I was beginning to erect the structure on which I could build and direct my future.

The meeting between Don and my parents was a disaster. They did not approve of my choice. Likewise, his parents did not approve of me. We could have mounted another rebellion and defied both sets of parents, but there was too much love and too many family ties that rivaled the love we had for each other. And what kind of a future could we build over the wreckage of heartbreak for both families? For once I "conformed" and abided by my parents' wishes. Don and I parted. It wasn't easy, but I was the richer for having known him. My husband and I hear from Don at Christmas time. He is the happy grandfather of many adoring grandchildren.

I made an emotional return to the scene of my first duty station, Newton D. Baker. It was pretty much as I had left it a year ago. My paraplegic boys were still there, some looking a bit healthier having filled out with much needed weight. I saw Robby again. He was the young man with a baby son sired before his disasterous injury. Hanging from one of the trapeze bars above his bed was the photograph of his baby in the silver frame I had bought on one of my trips to Baltimore.

I found the young tanker in the plastic surgery ward. I was interested to see how the skin grafts had taken on his hands. I was holding a hand and rubbing my thumb over the graft on the back of it. He jerked his hand away in mock offense and, in a high falsetto, he said, "Don't! That's my leg!" (the skin on his hand had been taken from his leg.) He hadn't lost his sense of humor. He and the rest of them had several years of painful treatment ahead of them. I marveled at how most of them could bear up with humor and optimism. I did not see the lad with no face. I returned home sober with the realization that these soldiers who had sacrificed their youth and put their futures on hold, in a flash, had had their lives changed forever.

In the fall of 1946, I enrolled at Kent State University in Kent, Ohio. I was taking advantage of the G.I. Bill of Rights whereby tuition and a small living stipend were paid by the government. The tremendous influx of veterans, seeking to prepare for a civilian career, strained the facilities of the colleges. G.I.'s without desks sat on the floor. Some classes were standing room only. The professors did not know how to handle the veteran students, many of whom were hardbitten, battle-scarred, tough ex-soldiers who had no compunction about challenging them. The professors were accustomed to eighteen year old incoming freshmen who accepted the lecture contents unquestioningly.

Lady vets were not as common then, and every time I got into a veterans' queue during the registration process, I was directed to the "regular" students' line. I was being registered as a freshman and told that I must take gym. It was compulsory. I objected. I had fulfilled my requisite gym classes the first time around as a freshman at Akron University. Given my recent army experiences, I had not grown soft in the interim.

I had sent for my Akron University and Akron City Hospital transcripts. The university credits were transferable, but nurses training credits had never been considered before. I called on the Registrar, submitted my nursing credits and asked him how much he would give me on them toward my degree. This was establishing a precedent. The full qualifying committee met which resulted in their giving me enough credit, so that coupled with my two years worth at Akron University, I could enter school on the senior level.

The four and five year degree programs for nurses had not come into being then. In fact, the face of nursing has changed so drastically that I am not sure but that there should be a redefinition of terms regarding the nurse.

The following story illustrates a terrible put-down to those of us who saved many, many lives without today's equipment, technology and medications: I was a patient on a diagnostic cardiac care ward. It was 11 PM at shift change. A young recent graduate appeared and flung herself down in a chair and began a conversation with the patient in the other bed. She was saying, "You know those old time graduates? All they ever did was look glamorous and go around giving back rubs." I bristled at this young woman's thoughtless remarks that would negate the accomplishments of my generation often under conditions beyond the scope of her imagination or experience. I was aghast at her unprofessionalism and the inappropriateness of her behavior. We are the pioneers that went before her and her colleagues, and in the service, we are the pioneers that went before today's service women. And I have not forgotten the pioneers that paved the way for me and my generation. I am proud to join the ranks of all the brave women that went before me.

I plunged into my studies with a vengeance. On week-ends, I worked nights at the Akron hospital, returning to Kent for Monday classes. I was career oriented. I didn't want any more men in my life. I did not date. I was a four-point student.

During this time, a small incident occurred that, ultimately, loomed large in my future. It has become part of the family legend: It was a balmy fall day. It seemed as if every veteran enrolled in school was lounging on the broad, park-like front lawn of the campus. It was noon and they were taking a picnic break with box lunches. A diagonal walk bisected the lawn. I was hurrying up the walk to a building some distance away for my noon class. My clothing was not very appealing - I was clad in the skirt of dubious green that the Japanese tailor had made and an old beige sweater set left over from high school - but that did not deter the assemblage from erupting with hoots and whistles and catcalls. I never knew quite how to handle that kind of attention. My first impulse was to tip my nose in the air and hurry on. On this occasion, I told myself not to be snooty. They were just having fun. I stopped and said something inane like, "Hello. It's a lovely day isn't it?"

In the throng was a young veteran who nudged his roommate and said, " See that girl? That's the girl I'm going to marry. ".…… and he did.

I wish I could tie up all the loose ends. I can mention only a few. I have mentioned Don and Janie elsewhere in this story. I still see Clenie and Schmitty. They are both widows now. Schmitty is in fragile health.* Clenie accompanied my husband and me to Washington D.C. on October 1997 for the dedication of the Women in Military Service of America Memorial located in Arlington Cemetery.

I still meet annually with many of my classmates at the Akron City Hospital Alumnae dinner. Most are veterans with experiences as varied as our numbers. They are a strong, beautiful, contributing group of women. I am very fortunate to count them among my friends. Despite the onslaught of disruptions that visit those of our generation, we succumb to our mastectomies, heart surgeries, shingles, broken bones and cancer only long enough to survive those episodes before we're off and running again.

We were highly disciplined in nurses training, and 'though we griped about it, we were very proud of the training we got. I am a champion of discipline, and that includes self-discipline. We are all subjected to the vagaries of life with its joy and sorrow, life and death, illness and robust health. Without discipline, we don't make it through the bad times. Without it, there would be no ballerinas, no scientists, no athletes, no musicians, no participants in any field of endeavor. It is hard for me to see my beloved America failing in so many of her principles because of a breakdown in discipline and a forfeiture of integrity and a depletion of the stuff from which backbones are made.

* As my story goes to print, I mourn the loss of Schmitty, my friend. She died peacefully in her sleep on June 23, 1998. She had been unable to be with us on our annual alumnae banquet, June 19, 1998. My concern for her prompted me to mail a manuscript to her rather than wait for the printed book. Schmitty

died the day I mailed the manuscript. She will be missed........

I have finished what I started out to do, that is to write my story about a very special time in my life. There is nothing that compares to the bond that binds those of us in uniform who shared the same life event; acted in concert to stem a grave crisis; rose to heights of heroism, sacrifice, and dedication beyond what mere man thought possible. No fraternity or sorority, lodge, secret society or cult, and even oft'times marriages have a more solid bond. The experience brings out the best in us and the worst in us. War strips us down to bare threads, and we see mankind's degradation and obscenity. We also see him rise to the heights with a kind of love that transcends life itself.

I have heard it said that things like patriotism, love and loyalty are obsolete. More's the pity if that is true. We need the nobler emotions in our lives to inspire us, to urge us on to the kind of spirituality that produces a great symphony, an enduring masterpiece, a miraculous medical discovery, or a workable prescription for peace. We cannot demand less of ourselves than we do of a gallant steed, or a faithful loving pet, or an enduring, patient beast of the fields. We have the capacity for greatness. How criminal to subvert our exalted potential and demand less than we can give.

I have come full circle evolving from idealism to cynicism and back to idealism. I have not given up on my fellow man. I have seen too much kindness, generosity, and decency to drown in the morass of social ills. It is another kind of war that we wage today, and one that will never be won unconditionally. It is the classic fight between good and evil, but it is worth our very best to stay the course.

And finally, I thought that I had lived my life without regrets until I got into the telling of this story. Dipping into the past forced me to open secret doors and confront all my yesterdays, but in so doing, I am reliving those moments from the perspective of today's maturity, and I see how I could have done things differently. Yes, I am rueful about a lot of things.

It is nobody's business but my own, but for those who are curious, this is the answer to the question; Did I keep my self-imposed vows of chastity? Yes.

Would I do it all again? You bet! In a hic-cup!

And, at the end, when I am embarking on the last great adventure of life, I hope I can summon a twinkle to my eye as I say to my beloved, "I've loved every minute of it!"

"Ah has spoken!"[23]

Clenie and I spent idyllic days hiking the Allegheny Mountains on our own private "R and R".

From left, Merideth and Jim Matthews of Akron share a laugh with Imez Myers of Reynoldsburg yesterday before the dedication of the Women in Military Service for America Memorial in Arlington, Va.

Female vets get place of honor

• Thousands attend dedication of memorial at Arlington National Cemetery

ANDREW MOULTON
Knight Ridder Newspapers

ARLINGTON, VA.: Their sacrifices were consigned to historical obscurity for years, but female veterans finally had their day yesterday as a memorial was dedicated to them on the nation's most hallowed ground: Arlington National Cemetery.

Under a gray sky in chilly weather, thousands of female veterans and military personnel gathered to dedicate the Women in Military Service for America Memorial, honoring the sacrifice of 1.8 million veterans and the more than 200,000 women who now serve.

Before an estimated 30,000 onlookers, World War I Navy yeoman Frieda Mae Hardin recounted her pioneering days in the military and challenged young women who are interested in military careers to "go for it."

"In my 101 years of living, I have observed many wonderful achievements, but none as important or as meaningful as the process of women taking their rightful place in society," she said.

The theme of honoring the past by pursuing equality in the future was a common thread for senior military and government speakers. Vice President Al Gore said the memorial is long overdue and should be a symbol of the nation's renewed commitment to combat sexism.

"In dedicating this memorial, let us be dedicated to root out intolerance and prejudice wherever they may exist," Gore said. "The women we honor today demand no less than full success in this mission."

Gore and other speakers avoided any direct references to the sexual harassment problems plaguing the military. But the meaning of Defense Secretary William Cohen's words were clear when he pledged that the military would "treat everyone in uniform with dignity and respect" and "hold accountable those who abuse their power."

Cohen said the new memorial serves as a challenge to uphold that pledge to women, who make up about 11 percent of military personnel.

The first female space shuttle pilot, Air Force Lt. Col. Eileen Collins, said her success was built on the contributions of female veterans who labored unlauded until now.

"I have observed an optimistic trend (in equality in the military) – not just more opportunities, but also more acceptance," Collins said.

The crowd flooded the drive leading to the cemetery's main gate, which faces the Lincoln Memorial across the Potomac River. The polished memorial's facade had languished as an incomplete, semicircular wall begun during the Depression; it was renovated with $9.5 million in tax dollars.

In the center of the semicircle is a 60,000-gallon reflecting pool.

Private donations paid for the excavation of 3,500 truckloads of dirt from behind the wall, making room for a 35,000-square-foot indoor space for an educational center. It includes a 196-seat theater, 14 exhibit alcoves, a conference center and a Hall of Honor.

About 250,000 women are entered in a computerized registry.

In our ancient uniforms, we participated fully in the WIMSA dedication, Oct. 1997. (Photo used with permission of Charles Kennedy, Knight-Ritter/Tribune)

END NOTES

1. (pg.2) - Scarlett O'Hara; Heroine in "Gone With The Wind" by Margaret Mitchell.

2. (pg.5) - "Toonerville Folks"; Cartoon by Mr. Fontaine Fox of Louisville, Ky.

3. (pg.7) - Lifebuoy; The trade name of antibacterial and antiodor soap.

4. (pg.15) - Maelstrom; Whirlpool off Norwegian coast described by Edgar Allen Poe.

5. (pg.16) - Gomer Pyle; Stumble-bum soldier in CBS comedy, "Gomer Pyle" 1964-1969.

6. (pg.17) - "Innocents Abroad"; Novel by Mark Twain.

7. (pg.22) - Hoover; Trade name of vacuum cleaner made by company of the same name in Canton,Ohio.

8. (pg.23) - "Laverne and Shirley"; Television situation comedy, 1976 - 1983.

9. (pg.24) - Shellshock; term from W.W. I; Battle fatigue term from W.W.II; Post Traumatic Stress Syndrome term from Vietnam War. All the forgoing are changes in terminology for the same syndrome.

10. (pg.31) - "The Little Engine That Could"; Childrens' book by Katy Piper.

11. (pg.40) - "Sentimental Journey"; Song from 1944, written by Les Brown, Ben Homer and Bud Greer.

12. (pg.46) - "Vogue"; Title of long running fashion magazine that is still in print.

13. (pg.49) - Lister; Name of English physician, Sir Joseph Lister, founder of aseptic surgery.

14.(pg.50) - Sir Walter Raleigh; English military and naval commander in the 16th and 17th century. Legend tells of his throwing his cloak over a puddle to protect the feet of Queen Elizabeth I.

15.(pg.58) - Pied Piper; Magician of legend who piped the children of Hamlin out of town when the townspeople reneged on payment for his services of ridding the town of rats. Hence, anyone who attracts a following of children.

16.(pg.61) - Stormtroopers; Name given to Hitler's dreaded SS Troops, sometimes called the killing squads.

17.(pg.71) - Odyssey; Homer's epic poem describing the ten year's wandering of Odysseus in returning to Ithaca after the Trojan Wars.

18.(pg.74) - Rembrandt; 17th century Dutch painter and etcher known for his use of light and shadow.

19.(pg.111) - Fates; Greek goddesses from classical Greek mythology who precided over destinies.

20.(pg.111) - Harpy; Evil winged monster from mythology.

21.(pg.117) - Lady Bountiful; Philanthropic character in "Beau Stratagem" by George Farquhar in 1707.

22.(pg.145) - Desert Storm; Code name of 1991 war with Iraq.

23.(pg.150) - "Ah has spoken!"; Pronouncement by Mammy Yokum, hillbilly matriarch of the Yokum family in Al Capp's "Li'l Abner", cartoon

ARMY SERVICE FORCES
Headquarters, Fifth Service Command
Fort Hayes, Columbus 18, Ohio

6 January 1945.

Miss Meredith Miller,
185 N. Firestone Blvd.,
Akron, Ohio.

My dear Miss Miller:

Inclosed are applications for you to fill out in duplicate and return to this office. When we are in receipt of these applications, we shall then proceed with your assignment to active duty.

Sincerely yours,

ALICE C. MERCHANT,
Capt, AUS, ANC,
Asst to SvC Surgeon.

ARMY SERVICE FORCES
Headquarters, Fifth Service Command
Fort Hayes, Columbus 18, Ohio

29 January 1945.

Miss Meredith J. Miller,
185 Firestone Blvd.,
Akron, Ohio.

My Dear Miss Miller:

This is to inform you that **you are physically qualified
for active duty in the Army Nurse Corps.**

It is therefore requested that you make whatever arrangements may be necessary in order to comply with orders when issued assigning you to active duty **on or about 1 March 1945.**

The salary for a nurse is $150, and $21 for food, per month. Upon your arrival at your first Station you will receive your clothing allowance of $250.

You are allowed 150 pounds of baggage on your railroad ticket. It is necessary to take two sets of bed linen, sheets, towels and pillow cases. Take only enough civilian street clothing as is necessary for one change.

Please reply by return mail, stating whether or not the above date is satisfactory; also, verify the address from which you wish to depart for active service.

Sincerely yours,

Alice C. Merchant
Capt. Army Nurse Corps,
Asst to SvC Surgeon.

ARMY SERVICE FORCES
Headquarters, Fifth Service Command
Fort Hayes, Columbus 18, Ohio

1 March 1945

Subject: Temporary Appointment.

To   :   2d Lt Meredith J Miller, AUS (ANC)   A   N-768837
            185 N. Firestone Blvd
            Akron, Ohio

1. By direction of the President you are temporarily appointed and commissioned a second lieutenant in the Army of the United States, effective this date for assignment to the Army Nurse Corps. Your serial number is shown after A above.

2. This commission will continue in force during the pleasure of the President of the United States for the time being, and for the duration of the war and six months thereafter unless sooner terminated.

3. There is inclosed herewith a form for oath of office which you are requested to execute and return promptly to the agency from which it was received by you. The execution and return of the required oath of office constitute an acceptance of your appointment. No other evidence of acceptance is required.

4. This letter should be retained by you as evidence of your appointment as no commissions will be issued during the war.

BY COMMAND OF MAJOR GENERAL COLLINS:

J. W. FRASER
Colonel, AGD,
Adjutant General.

I DO SOLEMNLY SWEAR . . .

"I, JANE DOE, having been appointed a second lieutenant, Army of the United States, do solemnly swear (or affirm) that I will support and defend the Constitution of the United States against all enemies, foreign or domestic, that I will bear true faith and allegiance to the same; that I take this obligation freely, without any mental reservation or purpose of evasion; and that I will well and faithfully discharge the duties of the office upon which I am about to enter; SO HELP ME GOD."

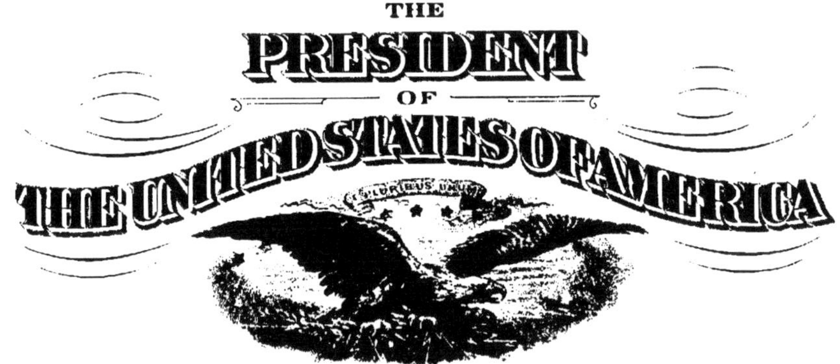

To all who shall see these presents, greeting:

Know Ye, that reposing special trust and confidence in the patriotism, valor, fidelity and abilities of ___Meredith Jeannette Miller___,

I do appoint him, temporarily, ___First Lieutenant___,

_______________________________ *in*

The Army of the United States

such appointment to date from the ___twenty-eighth___ *day of* ___April___, *nineteen hundred and* ___forty-six___ *He is therefore carefully and diligently to discharge the duty of the office to which he is appointed by doing and performing all manner of things thereunto belonging.*

And I do strictly charge and require all Officers and Soldiers under his command when he shall be employed on active duty, to be obedient to his orders as an officer of his grade and position. And he is to observe and follow such orders and directions, from time to time, as he shall receive from me, or the future President of the United States of America, or the General or other Superior Officers set over him, according to the rules and discipline of War.

This Commission to continue in force during the pleasure of the President of the United States, for the time being and for the duration of the present emergency and for six months thereafter unless sooner terminated.

Done at the City of Washington, this ___sixteenth___ *day of* ___May___ *in the year of our Lord one thousand nine hundred and* ___forty-seven___, *and of the Independence of the United States of America the one hundred and* ___seventy-first___.

By the President:

Major General,
The Adjutant General.

Army of the United States

CERTIFICATE OF SERVICE

This is to certify that

MEREDITH J MILLER N 768 837 1st. Lt.

334 Station Hospital

honorably served in active Federal Service
in the Army of the United States from

1 March 1945   to   20 May 1946

Given at   SEPARATION CENTER   Fort Sheridan Illinois

on the   20th   day of   May   1946

C. J. [illegible]
MAJOR, AGD

To you who answered the call of your country and served in its Armed Forces to bring about the total defeat of the enemy, I extend the heartfelt thanks of a grateful Nation. As one of the Nation's finest, you undertook the most severe task one can be called upon to perform. Because you demonstrated the fortitude, resourcefulness and calm judgment necessary to carry out that task, we now look to you for leadership and example in further exalting our country in peace.

Harry Truman

THE WHITE HOUSE